THE EMPTY PRISON CELL

THE EMPTY PRISON CELL

The Authenticity of Philemon Reconsidered

by

CHRIS M. HANSEN

WIPF & STOCK · Eugene, Oregon

THE EMPTY PRISON CELL
The Authenticity of Philemon Reconsidered

Wipf & Stock
An Imprint of Wipf and Stock Publishers
199 W. 8th Ave., Suite 3
Eugene, OR 97401

www.wipfandstock.com

PAPERBACK ISBN: 978-1-6667-8499-2
HARDCOVER ISBN: 978-1-6667-8500-5
EBOOK ISBN: 978-1-6667-8501-2

VERSION NUMBER 061724

To Gabby

My partner in crime

I thank my God always when I remember you in my prayers
—Philemon 4

Contents

Acknowledgments

THIS VOLUME IS THE product of my own amateur enthusiasm. I am a hobbyist when it comes to biblical studies, although I have, as of late, felt good enough about my work to share it openly. As a result, I have been published in a number of academic journals on early Christian history and New Testament studies, such as the *Journal of Early Christian History* and the *Journal of Greco-Roman Christianity and Judaism*. But again, I am and will remain an enthusiast for the most part. I do not specialize in biblical studies (I study English writing and literature), and as such I expect most will (and should) defer to subject experts on these matters. I frame this work not so much as something I expect to convince academics, but as the musings and ramblings of one C. M. E. Hansen.

Philemon has become a special interest to me. It is the shortest of Paul's letters and, in my opinion, the most curious. While studying other topics, primarily the Dutch Radicals, I came across their arguments against the authenticity of Philemon and was, surprisingly, convinced by some of their work. I endeavored at that point to learn more and see if anyone had attempted to rebut them, but I all found against critics of Philemon's authenticity was a lot of handwaving. Philemon's authorship does not seem to be a matter most people care to investigate for themselves. This air of dismissiveness and incuriosity (alongside my friend Joseph A. P. Wilson challenging me to formulate a coherent case against Philemon) sparked my interest in reviving the thoughts of past scholars whom I believe did not receive their due process.

While writing this, several people helped me track down sources and gave me plenty of criticism to mull over. The most notable of these are people I consider dear friends and colleagues: Joseph A. P. Wilson and Shannon Scott. Without their help, this volume would not have been made. I would also like to thank Jon DePue and Laura Robinson, whose stimulating conversations on various issues regarding authenticity, style, and methodology gave me much to reflect upon and greatly influenced my thought process while developing this volume. I must thank Gabby Bourgeois, my partner, for having put up with endless ranting and talk of an epistle they have never read, proofreading this text, and even helping with some of the research. This project would be a mess of epic proportions without them. They have the patience of twenty men and the endurance of an Olympic athlete. I also thank Seth M. Ehorn, Isaac T. Soon, Markus Vinzent, Mark G. Bilby, and a great many others for their encouragement and help in producing this volume.

Of course, all errors remaining are my own.

Chris M. Hansen
27 March 2024

A Content Warning

I WISH TO MAKE this note so readers are aware that this volume cites and pulls from authors who are less than reputable in terms of character. Some of them have outwardly displayed bigoted and oppressive behavior, which is inexcusable and which we as modern academics should not let go unchallenged.[1] As simply striking these figures from the record would be misleading, serve to undermine this volume's concerted effort at comprehensiveness, and make some research all but impossible to conduct, I have begrudgingly opted to include them. However, I wish to make it known that I fully condemn their actions and associations. I stand firmly with marginalized communities in making it clear that this behavior is not acceptable nor tolerable in the field of New Testament studies.

---

1. E.g., Price, *Holy Fable*, 1:151–54, which uses racist caricature and parody of American slavery in his description of Onesimus.

Introduction

I come from a family of missionaries. My mom's father went to Africa as a missionary in the 1990s, then to Mexico in the 2000s. Beyond that, he was a Gideon his entire life, a preacher, and a student of theology in his own conservative, Evangelical way. My dad's family was even more involved in missionary activity; my second great grandfather Jens Peter Hansen (1872–1903) came from Denmark, where he had been raised in a confined and stagnated Danish National Church in the town of Neder Randlev. His own experience was awful. He wrote:

> When in winter time, we did go to church we had to walk a long way, and as it was customary not to have fire in the church, I confess the two hours of service, sitting in a cold church with our feet on the stone floor and forced to sit as in the stillness of death, made Christianity (?)[1] seem rather hard. The whole affair was done more as a duty than for real worship, and it was so formal that little impression for good was made. The priest was considered (at least he considered himself) so far above common men, there was but little affection or sympathy shown, but he got his wages and lived in luxury, while the poor were oppressed. Experimental salvation was never heard of; didn't know there was such a thing, but was told to grow better, and though with a desire to do so, evidence proved we were all the time growing worse.[2]

After reaching America in the spring of 1891, Grandpa Peter (as the family affectionately calls him) converted to the Pentecost Bands, which at the time was loosely connected to the Free Methodist Church. Having been founded some years previously by Vivian A. Dake and with the blessing

1. Punctuation is original.

2. From Peter Hansen's autobiographical sketch entitled "From Bondage to Liberty" (ca. 1902). Document in possession of the Hansen family.

of the FMC's founder, B. T. Roberts, the Pentecost Bands spread with one mission: evangelizing the whole world. Peter Hansen became one of these missionaries. In 1894, Peter would write for *The Pentecost Herald* the following letter from his latest station in New Point, Indiana:

> We opened up meeting in this place March 24. We have a large hall and it is crowded every night. The Lord is with us and we expect wonderful things from Him. He is helping us to keep down and I feel the worth of souls as never before. I am so glad God's light overcame to my soul. I love this clear way with all my heart and I expect by God's help to live and die at my post. (April 1894)

He would, in time, get his wish, but before then Peter Hansen served as a missionary across the entire Midwestern United States. He married a fellow missionary, Ina Belle Cone, in 1899, and together they traveled abroad to Denmark, Norway, and Sweden with their companion Bessie Swanson to spread the Word. They returned in 1902 as Peter's health was failing and Ina was a few months pregnant with their first (and only) child. Peter Hansen at this point was suffering from terminal tuberculosis, but he continued to work, traveling all over the States and helping new missionaries like Fred Siefkin (later an FMC minister in Illinois) to find their ground. When he passed away on April 3, 1903, his last words were reportedly, "Glory to God, Glory to God . . . Amen."[3] His son, Win, later became a preacher in the FMC, traveling across the nation to aid in building congregations and churches down on their luck. Beyond this, my mother's parents traveled to Africa doing missionary labor, my own parents did missionary work in Jamaica and Egypt, my sister in Arizona, and I myself wound up street preaching with church members and going about "winning souls" (as Peter and Ina would have said) for Christ, though I do not do so anymore. I could expound for days on the lives of my grandfathers and grandmothers, but that is an entirely different project.

This is all to say that the legacy of missionary work has colored my life since childhood. Growing up, I knew few things about my family history, but I knew that Grandpa Peter was a missionary from Denmark. It is no surprise, then, that from an early age I developed a keen interest in the writings of Paul and stories of Christian missionaries from the first centuries. Their trials and work to convert the masses, and the oft-grisly fates they (supposedly) met, became focal points of my religious experience. But one

---

3. I published a lengthy article outlining his life, which also contains photographs of the movement and family. See Hansen, "From Rags to Reverend."

text that always stuck out to me, even way back then, is Philemon. The smallest of all of Paul's letters is the one I find to be an endless source of fascination. It is a personal letter, unlike the usual letters to congregations that Paul established or taught, yet it contains many rulings, attitudes, and notions that would become so important for Christians down the road, both for good and ill. Out of the thirteen Pauline letters, this one small letter has one of the most storied legacies.

INTRODUCTION TO THE ISSUE

Philemon's traditional narrative is one of the most recognizable early Christian stories among today's Christians. The story of the slave Onesimus being converted by the imprisoned apostle Paul and sent back to his master (which is now colloquially portrayed as Paul demanding his emancipation but was historically seen as a narrative about master/slave reconciliation) is a mainstay of Christian preaching and sermonizing today; the effect that this letter has had on the way Christians view the institution of slavery simply cannot be understated.

Perhaps in one of its most horrid chapters in history, Philemon was seen as outright justification for the enslavement of African Americans in the United States, with writers of the time noting that this letter had no apparent goal of advocating for emancipation or any change in the status of slaves whatsoever.[4] This, of course, comes as a shock to many modern Christians, who have likely overlooked it half a dozen times while flipping through their own Bibles. In reality, the single-page letter has been seen through most of Christian history as reaffirming the institution of slavery; early interpreters are virtually univocal about finding in it Paul's permission to own and use slaves.[5] Although letter has been interpreted as a message of both emancipation and oppression, the latter is by far the older and more infamous reading.

In short, Philemon has had a tumultuous relationship with its Christian readership. The reception history, however, is not the only reason for its importance. In other discussions, Paul's imprisonment (possibly in Rome[6]) mentioned in the letter often features among other prison epistles

4. Shalev, *American Zion*, 171.

5. Paley, "Questioning the Pauline Authorship of Philemon," 20.

6. This has been a source of endless debate for the last few centuries. Was the imprisonment in Ephesus? Colossae? Rome on the first occasion? Were there, perhaps, two

when discussing the supposed persecution of Christians in the first century. Much of this is to build up cases, such as by Sean McDowell. In his view, the apostles likely suffered and were martyred for their belief in Jesus, proclaiming the truth under torture. Their sincerity when recounting Jesus' resurrection should be taken as a sign of the story's truth.[7] To some, Philemon has become important to advancing current Christian apologia in this regard, as it stands as supposed evidence of this persecution complex.

For these reasons, I am in curious territory when challenging the authenticity of this letter, which is considered unassailable by almost all modern scholarship. Originally, I had no intention of even writing a study on this topic. For a long while, I had privately considered the letter likely inauthentic (following the works of the Dutch Radicals primarily, which I will touch on below) and that was that. However, in 2023 I was challenged by a good friend of mine, Dr. Joseph A. P. Wilson, to justify this case. After all, one cannot simply presume the inauthenticity of a letter no more than one can simply assume authenticity. It must be demonstrated. What initially began as a project for a simple article rapidly outgrew its confines. I would write into the early hours of the morning and then find I was thousands of words in and only just finished with my introductory topics. And now here you are, reading this volume, wherein I challenge a letter that virtually every scholar considers unchallengeable.

In this short volume, I will contend that the problem of Philemon's authenticity is not only questionable, but, at best, likely unresolvable. At worst, I find it likely to be inauthentic with a close relationship to other dubious letters, like Colossians and Ephesians. But first, it is important to contextualize this study.

THE QUESTION: A BRIEF OVERVIEW

The authenticity of the Pauline epistles has been continuously questioned for centuries now. While not often commented upon, Philemon did not have complete and universal acceptance in early Christian circles. We find, for instance, that in at least two manuscripts of Paul's letters—those being P46 (the oldest extant collection of Paul's letters) and Vaticanus—Philemon

---

imprisonments in Rome? In the end, the only person who knows the historical context of all these letters is one who has been dead for two thousand years.

7. McDowell, *Fate of the Apostles*, 94.

is not accounted for at all.[8] The Syrian church did not initially include Philemon either, considering it to be either lacking utility or wholly inauthentic from what we can tell.[9] Ephrem the Syrian's commentaries on the Pauline epistles notably exclude Philemon. Similarly, we are aware of some Christians during the time of some later church fathers who did not include Philemon in their canons for similar reasons as the Syrians, which resulted in said fathers defending the letter themselves.[10] Irenaeus seems aware of the entire Pauline corpus, save only Philemon, a trait also shared with Clement of Alexandria.[11] Thus, we can see that Philemon's authenticity was already being called into question during ancient times. However, the vast majority of Christians came to assert its authenticity, so Philemon became standard in various canon New Testaments. Unfortunately, the arguments that challengers posed in ancient times are now lost, and it is not until the burgeoning modern era that detailed arguments arose. Despite the acceptance of Paul's authorship of the letter, opinions were still far from complimentary; the superscript of one tenth-century manuscript describes Philemon as "trifling."[12]

Among the first challengers of the Pauline epistles in early modernity was Edward Evanson (1731–1805). In 1777 he began sharing doubts about the historical accuracy and genuineness of the New Testament corpus.[13] Later, in his *The Dissonance of the Four Generally Received Evangelists,* from 1792, he claimed that several of Paul's epistles were dubious; he took Acts to be the authoritative text that other epistles contradicted.[14] Regarding Philemon, Evanson claimed it inauthentic because it intimates that multiple prisoners were with Paul (Phlm 23), whereas Acts claims he was imprisoned by

8. See Walker, *Interpolations in the Pauline Letters,* 50–51n27; and Trobisch, *Paul's Letter Collection,* 20–21.

9. Tamez et al., *Philippians, Colossians, Philemon,* 201; Lohse, *Commentary,* 188; Williams, "'No Longer a Slave,'" 16.

10. Decock, "Reception of the Letter to Philemon," 277; and Heine, "In Search of Origen's Commentary on Philemon," 120. Both Decock and Heine emphasize that critics of Philemon's inauthenticity primarily focused on its lack of utility, though "that is one possibility entertained" (Heine, "In Search of Origen's Commentary on Philemon," 120).

11. Harding, "Disputed and Undisputed Letters of Paul," 133; Gallagher and Meade, *Biblical Canon Lists from Early Christianity,* 41.

12. Callahan, *Embassy of Onesimus,* 13.

13. Evanson, *Letter to the Right Reverend.*

14. See Detering, *Fabricated Paul,* 49–50 for an overview.

himself and kept by a guard (Acts 28:16).[15] Evanson's arguments have been largely lost to time, sadly.[16] Others, particularly anti-Christian polemicists, took to declaring that none of the Pauline epistles were authentic, such as Thomas Paine (1737–1809) in later editions of his *Age of Reason*.[17]

Most academics are primarily aware of the Tübingen School, led by Ferdinand Christian Baur (1792–1860), who argued that only the *Hauptbriefe* (1 and 2 Corinthians, Galatians, Romans) should be considered authentically Pauline.[18] Baur's criticisms of Philemon are the earliest detailed arguments against its authenticity that I am aware of. Presented in volume two of his *Paulus, der Apostel Jesu Christi, sein Leben und Wirken, seine Briefe und seine Lehre* (1845),[19] Baur's arguments are multifaceted. He first claims that all other prison epistles are of questionable authenticity (even Philippians). Then, he notes several linguistic features that either only appear in the disputed epistles or are unique to Philemon. He also observes that the letter is filled with several unlikely and coincidental events that can stagger belief when considered *in toto*. He then puts forth a counterinterpretation that sees the letter as a later commentary on Colossians. On this, he writes:

> If we understand Philemon as it must be understood, by not examining it merely on its own but instead looking at it in its historical-critical context together with the other epistles with which it belongs, then it is of course very problematic that people extol it especially for having no significance for the history of dogma or for church history, but just being an invaluable document for its excellent characterization of the Apostle Paul's amiable, sociable personality, and to a certain degree a practical commentary on Col 4:6. But even if it be a Pauline epistle.[20]

15. Evanson, *Dissonance*, 320. I use here the 1805 print by D. Walker.

16. Contemporary critics did not pretend to respond to his claims on Philemon. Joseph Priestley's response to Evanson's argument was to quote it and then state that it simply did not merit refutation; see Priestley, *Theological and Miscellaneous Works*, 455. For more on Evanson and his reception, see Van den Bergh van Eysinga, "Edward Evanson."

17. Paine, *Works of Thomas Paine*, section "Age of Reason," 197.

18. Detering, *Fabricated Paul*, 50–55. For a decent history of the school and Baur's influence, see Baird, *History of New Testament Research*, 258–78.

19. I am using here an English translation; see Baur, *Paul*, 305–8.

20. Baur, *Paul*, 308.

Few took to Baur's argumentation, though he did find a few contemporary allies; Bruno Bauer (1809–1882)[21] and other authors in the Dutch Radical tradition followed F. C. Baur's conclusions (below). Bruno Bauer himself died mostly in obscurity—a few Hegelian philosophers remembered him, but New Testament scholars by and large neglected his works.[22] More relevant were defenses from F. C. Baur's colleagues and students from the University of Tübingen, including his successor Karl Heinrich von Weizsäcker (1822–1899).[23] Von Weizsäcker theorized that Colossians and Philemon were written together by a post-apostolic author who perhaps belonged to a Pauline school of thought, making the Letter to Philemon "allegorical," according to his understanding. Another student of Baur's, Otto Pfleiderer, first viewed Philemon with suspicion, though by the 1870s his view had shifted completely.[24]

Aside from this, though, most other scholars added to the *Hauptbriefe* the letters of 1 Thessalonians, Philippians, and Philemon, to the chagrin of Baur and his followers. As such, these seven letters came to be accepted and stabilized over the nineteenth century and into the twentieth. This modified *Hauptbriefe* is still widely accepted to this very day, though some lively debate exists on whether to consider Ephesians and Colossians authentic while the Pastorals (1 and 2 Timothy and Titus) are broadly considered to be forgeries. Of course, this did not mean Philemon went unscathed. Heinrich Holtzmann (1832–1910), for instance, hypothesized that Philemon

21. Bauer, *Kritik der paulinischen Briefe*, 3:117, who accepts Baur's conclusions without much comment. Later citing Bauer was Bennett, *Gods and Religions of Ancient and Modern Times*, 1:714, who places Philemon in the dubious category.

22. In the Christ myth debate, renewed interest in Bauer was found. For instance, Evans, *Christ Myth*, 76 and 127 cited F. C. Baur and Bruno Bauer and was herself less than willing to grant authenticity to the Pauline epistles. Bauer had some influence on Marx and Engels. Engels, "On the History of Early Christianity," 331 claims the epistles (in their most current form) came about roughly sixty years after Revelation. Earlier (323–24) he cites both the Tübingen school (i.e. Baur and company) and Bruno Bauer. This claim later influenced Lenzman, *L'Origine du christianisme*, 43–44. Similarly, Kautsky, *Foundations of Christianity*, 18 states rather emphatically that no epistle is beyond dispute.

23. Von Weizsäcker, *Apostolic Age of the Church*, 244–45. Litton accused Heinrich Paulus of siding with Baur; see Litton, "Philemon." These radical views led to public outcry toward the university for its skeptical professors. For instance, Georg Heinrich Merz, who had studied at the University of Tübingen, reportedly decried the state of the university and its teachings on authenticity in the New Testament canon (see Zeller, "Charakteristik der modernen Bekehrungen").

24. Pfleiderer, *Urchristentums*, 683; cf. *Paulinismus*, 28 and *Primitive Christianity*, 1:263.

had several interpolations.[25] Similar to Holtzmann was Adolf Hausrath (1837–1909), who held that several portions of Philemon were interpolated with the same scribal malpractice he saw defacing Colossians.[26] More cautious was Wilhelm Brückner, though he still proposed verses 4–6 as un-Pauline interpolations due to their similarities with Colossians and Ephesians.[27] Few still argue this point today.[28] By and large, though, most academics considered the authenticity of Philemon unimpeachable.

Historically, secularist and freethought magazines and societies served as spaces for people to foster and air their doubts of the majority's consensus. In *The Agnostic* (a secularist magazine that circulated in England), a frequent contributor known only as "Julian" claimed that all Pauline epistles were forgeries of the mid-second century CE.[29] He claimed this prior to the spread of Dutch Radical thought and without apparent knowledge of Bruno Bauer; however, the reasoning behind his declaration was almost certainly polemical, i.e., in service to the author's virulent anti-Christian disposition.

The letter's reception was controversial for another reason: it was often interpreted as condoning the institution of slavery. The Rev. J. Colcock Jones remarked on a time he preached to slaves in Georgia:

> I was preaching to a large congregation on the Epistle to Philemon: and when I insisted on fidelity and obedience as Christian virtues in servants, and upon the authority of Paul, condemned the practice of running away, one-half of my audience deliberately rose up and walked off with themselves; and those who remained looked anything but satisfied with the preacher or his doctrine. After dismission, there was no small stir among them; some solemnly declared that there was no such Epistle in the Bible; others that it was not the Gospel; others, that I preached to please the masters; others, that they did not care if they never heard me preach again.[30]

25. Holtzmann, "Brief an den Philemon." Elsewhere, however, Holtzmann is less certain of Philemon; see Holtzmann, "Introduction to the Epistle to Philemon," 3:111–12.

26. Hausrath, *History of New Testament Times*, 122–23.

27. Brückner, *Chronologische Reihenfolge*, 200–203.

28. O'Neill, "Paul Wrote Some of All," 169 claims, "Paul wrote some of all, but not all of any of the epistles that bear his name; even Philemon was glossed." He does not, unfortunately, elaborate on this. Robertson, *Bible and Its Background*, 2:69 claims there were "one or two" possible interpolations but does not single out any passages.

29. Julian, "Popular Religious Faith," 32.

30. Quoted in Callahan, *Embassy of Onesimus*, 1.

The reasons here are clearly both theological and social. This White minister's sermon to African slaves declared that their legal status as property and draft animals was Christian virtue in disguise. The reaction was to reject the letter and reject the pastor who upheld it to further their oppression. The letter was a favorite among Southern clergy to promote white supremacy.

By the late nineteenth century, doubts about Philemon had largely evaporated in English, French, and German scholarship, although there remained a small contingent of academics that went beyond even Baur and his students. The Dutch Radicals were a group of scholars who were, as the name implies, predominantly localized in the Netherlands and known for their insistence that exactly zero Pauline epistles are authentic.[31] Headed by figures like Allard Pierson, Abraham Dirk Loman, Samuel Naber, and Gerardus Johannes Petrus Josephus Bolland, they promoted radical criticism of the New Testament, with several concluding Jesus never existed as a historical figure (though this was not universal among the Radicals). To them, the epistles were all late constructions of the second century CE, often seen as patchwork pieces littered with interpolations and stitched together from other letters and ideas by various groups polemicizing each other.[32] The Dutch Radicals, predictably, found few adherents beyond their own schools (predominantly the University of Leiden and University of Amsterdam), though a few individuals involved in the Christ myth debate took up their work (or modifications of it) in the name of proving Jesus a mythical figure.[33] Their most influential member outside of the Nether-

31. For an introduction to the Radicals, see Detering, "Dutch Radical Approach to the Pauline Epistles"; and Peabody, "H.J. Holtzmann and His European Colleagues." See also Detering, *Fabricated Paul*, 55–64; Detering, *Paulusbriefe ohne Paulus?*, passim and reprinted in *Inszenierte Fälschungen*, passim; Van den Bergh van Eysinga, *Radical Views About the New Testament*, passim. Brief introductions also exist in Verhoef, "Willem Christiaan van Manen"; "'Dutch Radicals' Espoused Historical Research"; "Holländische Radikale Kritik." For a more detailed overview, see Hagar, "Radical School of Dutch New Testament Criticism."

32. Pierson and Naber, *Verisimilia*; Loman, *Quaestiones Paulinae* (all parts cited in bibliography); Bolland, *Evangelische Jozua*.

33. For examples, see Johnson, *Antiqua Mater* and *Pauline Epistles* (where he promotes a strange conspiracy theory that most ancient history was forged by Benedictine Monks in the sixteenth century); Whittaker, *Origins of Christianity*, 67–216; Rylands, *Critical Analysis*; Drews, *Christ Myth*, 165–213 and *Witnesses to the Historicity of Jesus*, 61–65, 102–21; Kalthoff, *Rise of Christianity*, 142–53; Remsburg, *Bible*, 153–54 places Philemon in the "dubious" category; Cutner, *Jesus*, 30–57 is clearly unconvinced of any Pauline epistles' authenticity and cites Van Manen. Early socialist authors were somewhat

lands was Willem Christiaan van Manen (1842–1905), who published only a handful of English-language essays but became noteworthy after some were included in the 1902 *Encyclopaedia Biblica*.[34] Van Manen's own work rested on Baur's, though with a few notes taken from other academics as well; he seemingly relied in part on Rudolf Steck's work[35] and contended that Philemon was derived from Pliny the Younger's letters to Sabinianus (*Ep.* 9.21, 9.24), noting a number of curious parallels between the texts.[36] Notably, Van Manen also held that there are some linguistic peculiarities (such as this supposedly being the only "authentic" letter where Paul's himself a "prisoner"). From this, Van Manen also concluded that Philemon is inauthentic, likely written between 125 and 130 CE.

G. A. van den Bergh van Eysinga (1874–1957), a student of Van Manen, was one of the last in the initial wave of Dutch Radicals. He offered a tour de force of argumentation against the authenticity of Philemon in a 1940 article published in *Nieuw Theologisch Tijdschrift*,[37] for which there has been (to my knowledge) no rebuttal. This is unsurprising for several reasons. The article was released at the height of the Second World War, during which the Netherlands was occupied by Nazi forces. Additionally, only a small constituent of people could fluently read and interact with Dutch outside of Germany and the Netherlands, which meant that the works of the Dutch Radicals went almost entirely unnoticed outside of their native country. Despite these pitfalls, many of Van den Bergh van Eysinga's arguments, in my view, deserve closer attention. I will at points pull from his criticisms, which include useful summaries and additions in German from Hermann Detering (1953–2018).[38] Despite their ardent position that every Pauline epistle is inauthentic, other Radicals spent very little time on Philemon compared to Van Manen and Van den Bergh van Eysinga.

---

influenced by them as well; see Brown, *Communism and Christianity*, 186–88, who challenges the authenticity of virtually all the New Testament and cites Van Manen on Paul. The Radicals had some influence on Soviet scholars as well; see Kryvelev, *Christ*, 177–79.

34. These have been reprinted in Van Manen, *Wave of Hypercriticism*.

35. Van Manen himself had previously defended the authenticity of the *Hauptbriefe* and 1 Thessalonians, but he rescinded his views after reading Steck's radical volume challenging Galatians' authenticity; see Verhoef, "Willem Christiaan van Manen."

36. Van Manen, *Wave of Hypercriticism*, 149–51. See also Steck, "Plinius im Neuen Testament."

37. Van den Bergh van Eysinga, "Paulus' Brief aan Philemon."

38. Detering, *Paulusbriefe ohne Paulus?*, 332–36, reprinted in *Inszenierte Fälschungen*, 365–70.

Defenses of the authenticity of Philemon have historically been lack-
luster, often dismissing the issue with virtually no comment (sometimes
literally no comment). To date, I have found no serious attempt to defend
Philemon's authenticity in any major commentary on the epistle.[39] The few
defenses on offer are rather brief and inconsequential, either not engaging
with any points raised by Philemon's critics or, at most, only their weakest
ones.[40]

39. For older commentaries, see Vincent, *Critical and Exegetical Commentary*, 159–
60, who briefly discusses alternative views before dismissing them, stating, "It is needless
to waste time over these" including Baur; Erdman, *Epistles of Paul*, 127; Moule, *Epistles to
the Colossians and to Philemon*, 147–48; Ewald, *Briefe des Paulus*, 1–54 does not address
Baur's or other critics' complaints with Philemon; Müller, *Epistles of Paul to the Philippians and to Philemon*, 166–67 says, "it is only stubborn and prejudiced tendency criticism
which can doubt its genuineness" and little else; one of the lengthiest discussions I have
found is Lemaire, *Étude sur l'épître de S. Paul à Philémon*, 9–14. For recent commentaries,
see Barth and Blanke, *Letter to Philemon*, 130–31; Beale, *Colossians and Philemon*, 367;
Moo, *Letters to the Colossians and to Philemon*, 361; Dunn, *Epistles to the Colossians and to
Philemon*, 299–300; Lohse, *Colossians and Philemon*, 188; Bird, *Colossians & Philemon*, 4;
Kreitzer, *Philemon*, 1; Ehorn, *Philemon*, digital edition (unpaginated) dismisses the issue
noting Baur only as a challenger; Wilson, *Colossians and Philemon*, 317; Fitzmyer, *Letter
to Philemon*, 8–9; Tarazi, *Colossians & Philemon* assumes authenticity throughout; M.
Thompson, *Colossians and Ephesians*, 193; Wright, *Colossians and Philemon*, 168; Melick,
Philippians, Colossians, Philemon, 336; McKnight, *Letter to Philemon*, 37; Ebner, *Brief an
Philemon*, 4 just assumes authenticity (I found no reference to any challengers, not even
F. C. Baur); Müller, *Brief an Philemon*, 80 briefly notes Van Manen and Baur and then
dismisses the issue without defense; Barclay, *Colossians and Philemon*, 97; Bruce, *Epistles*,
192–93; Keegan, *First and Second Timothy, Titus, Philemon*, 67; Stuhlmacher, *Brief an
Philemon*, 19–20; Gnilka, *Philemonbrief*, 3–4; McDonald, *Commentary on Colossians &
Philemon*, 151; Gorday, ed., *Colossians*, 309; A. Thompson, *Colossians and Philemon*, 5;
Hahn and Mitch, *Ignatius Catholic Study Bible*, 409; Patzia, *Ephesians, Colossians, Philemon*, 10; Carter, *Pastoral Epistles*, 265; Pao, *Colossians & Philemon*, 341–42; Tamez et al.,
Philippians, Colossians, Philemon, 201 briefly discusses authenticity but largely assumes
it without retort; Verhoef, *Filippenzen, Filemon*, 93; O'Brien, *Colossians, Philemon*, 269;
Thompson and Longenecker, *Philippians and Philemon*, 151–52. Several never bother
addressing the issue; see these commentary introductions: Osiek, *Philippians and Philemon*, 125–31; Cousar, *Philippians and Philemon*, 95–98; Weidmann, *Philippians, First
and Second Thessalonians, Philemon*, 217–22; Migliore, *Philippians and Philemon*, 189–
200; Garland, *Colossians and Philemon*, 293–312; Suhl, *Brief an Philemon*, 9–24; Hamm,
Philippians, Colossians, Philemon, 27–60; Wall, *Colossians & Philemon*, 179–91. See also
the following papers : Head, "Onesimus the Letter Carrier," 630–31; Knox, "Philemon
and the Authenticity of Colossians," 145; Smith, "Later Pauline Letters," 304. Additionally, see Boring, *Introduction to the New Testament*, 230; Bernier, *Rethinking the Dates of
the New Testament*, 133; Brogdon, *Companion to Philemon*, xviii. Schweitzer's *Paul and
His Interpreters* at no point deals with Philemon's authenticity.

40. Bruce, *Epistles*, 192–93.

Curiously, one of the only defenses consistently offered for the authenticity of Philemon is a difficulty in imagining why someone would invent such a small and personal letter of this nature.[41] This very contention was something that Baur (and others) had already anticipated.[42] Despite this, it is not difficult to find commentators making pronouncements of such magnitude that they stretch credulity to its limits, such as McDonald claiming:

> The Pauline authorship of Philemon is beyond all reasonable doubt. It has early attestation. And the internal evidence is strong, for historical reality is stamped on every sentence of the letter. . . . Ernest Renan was right in his assertion that "few pages have so clear an accent of truth; Paul alone, it would seem, could have written this little masterpiece."[43]

I am sure it would be much to McDonald's annoyance that such skepticism does exist and is surely warranted. Few revivals of the inauthenticity thesis have shown up in contemporary times, but the exceptions are worth some review. The first was Hermann Detering in the 1992 publication of his PhD dissertation, entitled *Paulusbriefe ohne Paulus? Des Paulusbriefe in der holländischen Radikalkritik*. This volume was mainly an attempt at rejuvenating works of the Dutch Radicals, and though he took his arguments on Philemon primarily from Van den Bergh van Eysinga, he included hints of Baur, Steck, and Van Manen as well.[44] The arguments put on full display the linguistic peculiarities in Philemon, the odd narrative setting, and the similarities to Pliny's letter, alongside other notable issues. Shortly thereafter, Darrell J. Doughty and Robert M. Price began the *Journal of Higher Criticism*, and in its inaugural issue Doughty issued his own skepticism about the epistles and flirted with the Dutch Radical position.[45] A few years later, Detering would publish an article serving as an introduction to the Radicals.[46] Not long after that, Doughty translated Detering's more public-facing book into English as a supplement for the journal's tenth volume.[47]

---

41. Bruce, *Epistles*, 191.

42. Baur, *Paul*, 305.

43. McDonald, *Commentary on Colossians & Philemon*, 151.

44. Detering, *Paulusbriefe ohne Paulus?*, 332–36; reprinted in *Inszenierte Fälschungen*, 365–70.

45. Doughty, "Pauline Paradigms and Pauline Authenticity."

46. Detering, "Dutch Radical Approach to the Pauline Epistles."

47. Detering, *Fabricated Paul*.

Following from Van Manen, primarily, Robert M. Price has repeatedly iterated his own doubts about Philemon's authenticity. In his *Pre-Nicene New Testament: Fifty-Four Formative Texts* (2006), Price argues inauthenticity based exclusively on Philemon's close parallels with Pliny's letter to Sabinianus.[48] In his later volume, *The Amazing Colossal Apostle: The Search for the Historical Paul* (2012), Price added minimal discussion to this point in the form of Stephan Huller's thesis, which suggests that the letter was invented to "beef up the authority of Bishop Onesimus," who is mentioned in Ignatius, *Epistle to the Ephesians* 1–2, 6.[49] The most extensive argumentation offered thus far for Philemon's inauthenticity, however, comes from Günther Schwab's *Echtheitskritische Untersuchungen zu den vier kleineren Paulusbriefen* (2011, band 1, halbband A), which presents a complex series of literary and linguistic reasons to consider the epistle spurious.[50] Doughty, Schwab, Price, and Detering predominantly form what I have dubbed the *neo-Dutch Radical school* of thought, though this has since largely died out with the passing of Doughty and Detering, plus Schwab's inactivity in the field since publishing his PhD dissertation in 2011.[51] The neo-Radicals have found a few takers in the Christ myth debate, but not in larger academia.[52]

The most recent arguments for inauthenticity have come from Justin Paley, who released the article "Questioning the Pauline Authorship of Philemon: Crackpot Theory or Plausible Alternative?" in the *Expository Times* (2022). In this article, Paley observes numerous double standards applied

48. Price, *Pre-Nicene New Testament*, 467–68. Following this, Carrier, *On the Historicity of Jesus*, 261n12 is sympathetic to the inauthenticity of Philemon. Price has commented on this in other works as well; see *Holy Fable* 3:151–54 (wherein he also makes racist remarks parodying African American vernacular English and slavery in the American South). Price has hoped that his views would extend to encapsulate more of the Christ myth debate, contending that mythicists do not need an early date for the epistles; see Price, "Does the Christ Myth Theory Require an Early Date."

49. Price, *Amazing Colossal Apostle*, 502–4.

50. Schwab, *Echtheitskritische Untersuchungen zu den vier kleineren Paulusbriefen*, 87–199.

51. Hansen, "Evaluation of the Neo-Dutch Radical School" summarizes and rebuts some of the looser methodologies exhibited by Detering and Price.

52. E.g., Salm, *NazarethGate*, 400, 408, 434–44, 474; Skjønsberg, *Jesus Story*, 283–90. More recently and far more methodologically coherent has been Britt and Wingo, *Christ Before Jesus*, 241–44, who argue that Philemon was inauthentic on the following grounds: (1) personal letters have a propensity for being easier to fake; (2) overlap with Colossians; (3) the "signature" in verse 19 looks to be a forgery to throw off concerns of inauthenticity; (4) it appears to build the reputation of one bishop Onesimus. Their argumentation is largely influenced by Robert M. Price here.

in Pauline studies to exempt Philemon from the same criticism as other inauthentic epistles, such as Colossians and the Pastorals. Paley's article notes that its closest linguistic relationship is with Colossians, including various names and people, before listing other issues (such as scholars exempting Philemon from being considered inauthentic based on stylistic analyses, noting its brevity, while not doing the same for the Pastorals). Some of the core seven epistles besides Philemon have also been scrutinized, though their authenticity is still widely asserted.[53]

Despite the increasing number of challengers, defenders of Philemon are nearly impossible to find in the present day. Authenticity is frequently treated as a given, and believers often have derisive comments for the few who have challenged its legitimacy in the past. Personally, I think that skepticism about this letter is entirely warranted and that the authenticity of any Paulines should not be assumed. Hart notes that discussions of pseudonymity (discussed more below) and authenticity in the Pauline corpus largely start with the *Hauptbriefe*'s privileged status in our discourse, but that we may not need to start there and should perhaps challenge that privileged status instead.[54] Regarding reactions to the Dutch Radical school, we find that the consensus on Philemon's authenticity (and, in large part, the authenticity of most Pauline texts) is not due to scholars having ever truly interacted with and thoroughly disproven Radical viewpoints; as Price remarks (quoted by Hart), "It is not that the Dutch Radical critical paradigm

53. For recent skepticism, see McGuire, "Did Paul Write Galatians?"; Crüsemann, *Pseudepigraphal Letters to the Thessalonians*; O'Neill, *Paul's Letter to the Romans* and *Recovery of Paul's Letter to the Galatians*; Brodie, *Beyond the Quest for the Historical Jesus*, 137–54. In recent years a "neo-Dutch Radical" school has evolved among a few academics and the so-called "mythicist" crowd; see Detering, *Fabricated Paul, Inszenierte Fälschungen*, and "Dutch Radical Approach to the Pauline Epistles." Since the publication of Detering's PhD thesis, a micro neo-Dutch Radical school of thought emerged among a handful of academics and lay authors (largely in the context of the Christ myth debate); see Doughty, "Pauline Paradigms and Pauline Authenticity"; Price, *Amazing Colossal Apostle*; *Bart Ehrman Interpreted*, 93–109; *Holy Fable* 3:13–168; and *Pre-Nicene New Testament*, 315–480; Salm, *Nazareth Gate*, 400, 408, 434–44, 474; Zindler, *Jesus the Jews Never Knew*, 193; Skjønsberg, *Jesus Story*, 283–90. We will only mention a few of the more outlandish theories, such as that Paul wrote after the second temple was destroyed (Lawrence, *Seventy*) or the Roman provenance theories that posit the letters were fabrications of imperial Rome (Piso and Gallus, *Piso Christ*; Atwill, *Shakespeare's Secret Messiah*; Davis, *Creating Christianity*). See Hansen, "Popular History and Roman Provenance" for refutation of the Roman Provenance theories.

54. Hart, *Prolegomenon*, 102–3.

was tried and found wanting; it was found distasteful and not tried."[55] On that note, Maurice Goguel in his *Jesus the Nazarene* (originally published in 1925) wrote of the Dutch Radicals:

> The fact that they have failed to give from their point of view a coherent explanation of the origins of Christianity and of the formation of the Gospel tradition explains the slight influence that their theories have exercised.[56]

Notably, Goguel spends virtually no time discussing or evaluating their views at all. His two brief paragraphs of dismissiveness come without having ever evaluated the Radicals' theories and argumentation.[57] On a more caustic note, F. F. Bruce infamously remarked that the Radical theories of Van Manen were "hypercriticism" and "naïveté."[58] In reviewing the *Encyclopaedia Biblica*, H. N. Bate remarked that "Prof. van Manen writes on Philemon and Philippians, rejecting both Epistles on grounds which can hardly be called substantial," then fails to comment on Van Manen's actual arguments against authenticity.[59] More recently, we can point to Andreas J. Köstenberger, L. Scott Kellum, and Charles L. Quarles, who write of Baur's work (the only critic they cite), "His arguments against authenticity are now dismissed by virtually all scholars."[60] Lastly, Scot McKnight dismisses the entire discussion (without referencing a single critic) in one sentence: "Few scholars dispute Paul's authorship of Philemon."[61] This is usually all that is offered by leading commentators and scholars on Philemon: a conspiracy of silence, and an abject dismissal of criticism without serious engagement. It is a sign of a consensus built upon straw when no one can or is willing to mount a defense of said consensus, opting instead to assert

---

55. Price, *Amazing Colossal Apostle*, 40. Hart further elaborates on this in *Prolegomenon*, 103–6. Here, Hart (pulling from Arnal and McGann) notes that the Pauline corpus is not one that was transmitted unaltered from Paul's hands. It is instead a body of work that has undergone revision and refinement over time, not only in the form of interpolations, but interpretation, collection, order, and more. The text is far from stable to the extent we may, as Arnal (via Hart, *Prolegomenon*, 103) notes, side with the intuition that there is "something decidedly second-century, or even later, about this way of imagining Paul."

56. From the English translation, see Goguel, *Jesus the Nazarene*, 56.

57. Goguel, *Jesus the Nazarene*, 56.

58. Bruce, *Paul*, 396. Cf. Bruce, *Epistles*, 193.

59. Bate, "Chronicle," 308.

60. Köstenberger, Kellum, and Quarles, *Cradle, the Cross, and the Crown*, 623.

61. McKnight, *Letter to Philemon*, 37.

it as fact without question. A consensus of straw, then, is one that does not merit existence.

In short, there has been little to no fair attempt at evaluating theories the Radicals presented, and even to this day I can find no critical commentary in the English language that has set forth to comprehensively defend the authenticity of Philemon against the Radicals. Instead, if they are mentioned at all, they are simply handwaved away. I am not the only one to notice this; Luke Timothy Johnson in his *Constructing Paul* (2020) has likewise opined the treatment of letters like Colossians and Ephesians, while Philemon has escaped unscathed due to double standards.[62]

This is part of a broader trend Hart points out, where issues of authenticity regarding the seven-letter collection largely regarded as "authentic" are routinely brushed aside, if commented upon at all, especially where the *Hauptbriefe* are concerned.[63] Academics at large have habitually avoided discussing the authenticity of the general seven epistles, and especially not the *Hauptbriefe*, which are afforded an extra-special status of unimpeachability.. As a result, it is not surprising to find scholars like Bernier, who eschew all discussions of authenticity altogether with comments such as:

> I do not engage in the work of demonstrating or refuting the authenticity of the canonical Pauline letters. This study is already long enough without replicating such earlier work. Instead, I refer readers to relatively recent studies arguing in favor of the authenticity of various disputed works within the Pauline corpus.[64]

Note the key distinction is "disputed works," which are the only ones Bernier feels a need to recommend defenses for (i.e., those works that he cannot assert a consensus to defend). The other epistles, however (including Philemon), are simply assumed authentic. Bernier states, "scholars agree that Paul certainly contributed to Romans, 1 and 2 Corinthians, Galatians

---

62. Johnson, *Constructing Paul*, 248. Johnson, of course, does not give his own defense of Philemon but uses it as a pretense for the authenticity of Colossians and Ephesians. In discussing Philippians and Philemon, he makes several strange errors (notably to point out that Philippians has supposedly un-Pauline characteristics). For instance, he claims that Philippians has no scriptural citations (89). This is incorrect (Phil 2:15 cites Deut 32:5, for instance). His study noticeably lacks engagement with several leading works like Leppä, *Making of Colossians*; and Ehrman, *Forgery and Counterforgery*, which makes his discussions precarious in nature.

63. Hart, *Prolegomenon*, 110.

64. Bernier, *Rethinking the Dates of the New Testament*, 134.

Philippians, 1 Thessalonians, and Philemon."[65] This amounts to replicating and reifying the consensus position, which, as we have seen, has few means of propping itself up. To Bernier and others like him, the consensus is an entity that is automatically correct, and recent challengers of it are not worth mentioning. Even though there exist studies calling into question the seven canonized epistles that are just as recent as some of those Bernier cites on the Pastorals, they do not see the light of day in his (or other scholars') commentaries.[66]

There may be a few more reasons that Philemon escapes discussion. Perhaps the story is so culturally engrained and important that few feel comfortable challenging it. Although, more likely, as Seesengood writes, "One wonders if scholars haven't considered the question largely because they see less theological merit or value in Philemon."[67] Seesengood's somber comments, in my opinion, accurately reflect the situation and are borne out entirely by a review of most commentaries (see above) on Philemon:

> It is possible that Philemon made it into the canon largely because it carried the name of Paul and was deemed, frankly, too theologically insignificant to bother with elaborate arguments for or against its inclusion. In many ways, it may continue to find its Pauline authorship undisputed for exactly the same reasons.[68]

All of this is in spite of the fact that "There is just as much reason to challenge Pauline authorship of Philemon as there is to challenge Colossians or 2 Thessalonians."[69] My challenge to Philemon's authenticity, then, is more than warranted given this ongoing trend of outright ignoring the question. The consensus among academics is one of repetition, not erudition or coherent argumentation; scholars repeated the claim that Philemon is authentic until it became a fact in their minds, and because they frequently do little to no research on the topic of authenticity, the works of challengers have gone largely unnoticed. More recent work from Seesengood, which

---

65. Bernier, *Rethinking the Dates of the New Testament*, 133.

66. E.g., Crüsemann, *Pseudepigraphal Letters to the Thessalonians*; Brodie, *Beyond the Quest for the Historical Jesus*, 137–54; Detering, *Inszenierte Fälschungen*; Price, *Amazing Colossal Apostle*; Paley, "Questioning the Authorship of Philemon."

67. Seesengood, *Philemon*, 83.

68. Seesengood, *Philemon*, 83.

69. Seesengood, *Philemon*, 83.

does take serious issue with this consensus, does not mention any scholars who make arguments against Philemon's authenticity besides F. C. Baur.[70]

In this volume, I situate myself largely with the more radical tradition and attempt to give these positions the hearing they have been denied in New Testament scholarship. With this, others may come away with a view of Philemon that drastically differs from the current consensus.[71]

WHAT IS AUTHENTICITY?

It is important for us to consider what we mean when we ask whether a document is "authentic." Naturally, this raises other questions: What counts as pseudonymous? What is pseudonymity? More troublesome than this, what do we mean when we say that Paul wrote anything?

On these matters, I must acknowledge my indebtedness to Patrick Hart's *A Prolegomenon to the Study of Paul* (2020). According to Hart, pseudonymity takes on numerous forms in ancient texts and can be viewed in a variety of ways. We may see an entire single work as pseudonymous, or only a portion of it (interpolations), or perhaps entire letter collections themselves (this calls to mind the letters of the *Historia Augusta*, or the letters between Paul and Seneca).[72] Following Hart's reflection on the distinction of pseudonymity and pseudepigraphy, we must recognize that in questioning the authenticity of Philemon, we are not dealing with a pseudepigraph (a text that has been falsely attributed to someone but internally lacks the referent it is associated with).[73] Instead, we are working with the issue of pseudonymity, as Philemon claims (in verse 1) to have been at least coauthored by the apostle Paul.[74]

Pseudonymity has, as Hart describes, two broad categories: (1) the malicious form, wherein the pseudonymous author ascribes a text to an opponent in the hopes of either discrediting earlier work or disparaging

70. Seesengood, *Philemon*, 79–83.

71. To situate myself as "radical" is not a negative, as some take it to be. Instead, I use it in the sense that A. D. Loman (one of the Dutch Radicals) used it; i.e., that of rejecting the usual and standard ways of thinking about Christian origins and studying the New Testament, to be innovative and break the confines. See Verhoef, "Holländische Radikale Kritik," 427.

72. Hart, *Prolegomenon*, 85.

73. Hart, *Prolegomenon*, 90–91 looks at Hebrews as an example of a pseudepigraph; it was falsely attributed to Paul despite lacking any internally named referent author.

74. Timothy's involvement will be discussed below.

the whole of that person's work via association with a degrading letter;[75] the other category (2) is more affectionate and involves a disciple or admirer of the person being imitated ascribing authorship of a pseudonymous letter out of love or respect, effectively continuing that person's work. Hart provides Colossians, Ephesians, and 2 Thessalonians as often seen as examples of the latter category.[76] Hart discusses a potential third category, where an author may use pseudonymity to avoid unwanted attention.[77] We might also consider novelistic or fictional epistles a fourth category when attributed to a real person, though this is more complicated.[78]

This discourse comes with rather intense feelings; Hart discusses that New Testament scholarship is rife with internal "defense mechanisms" regarding the potential realities of pseudonymity. For instance, while it is known that pseudonymity often came with an intentionally deceptive element, New Testament scholars have frequently resisted this, insisting that "these forgeries were never meant to deceive anyone" in the New Testament.[79] The reasons for this are obvious, as devout Christians and those with Christian-like preoccupations would otherwise have to concede that there is literary deceit within the "canon" of the New Testament. Thus, they invent ways to mitigate this that do not involve acknowledging deceptive elements. Pseudonymity, then, stands as an inherent threat to the moral character of New Testament authors and the authority of Scripture itself, as Hart explains.

So, when speaking of pseudonymity, we could mean multiple things, and regarding Philemon, the issue is complicated further by the inclusion of Timothy as a coauthor. Most of Paul's works claim to be coauthored, and Timothy frequently appears in letters as another writer.[80] Thus, when

75. Hart, *Prolegomenon*, 93, quoting Clarke, notes the example of Diotimus the Stoic, who wrote a collection of "obscene" letters under Epicurus' name as a means of "tarnishing his character."

76. Hart, *Prolegomenon*, 95.

77. Hart, *Prolegomenon*, 95–96.

78. To be clear, there were many reasons why one may have forged a text that do not include malicious intent to deceive at all; see Soon, "Before Deception," and chapter 4 below.

79. Hart, *Prolegomenon*, 97.

80. The most common combination found is Paul and Timothy. 2 Cor 1:1 claims to be written by Paul and Timothy; Phil 1:1 lists Paul and Timothy as coauthors; Col 1:1 lists Paul and Timothy as coauthors; 1 Thess 1:1 lists Paul, Timothy, and Silas as all coauthoring the letter as does 2 Thess 1:1; Phlm 1:1 lists Paul and Timothy as coauthors. A few other coauthors are listed on occasion; see 1 Cor 1:1, which claims to be written by Paul

talking of authorship and what it means for Paul to be an author, we must remember that he is frequently a cowriter. In cases where Paul is listed as a singular author, we should acknowledge the potential hand of an amanuensis, who could have left their own flourishes and additions. In short, authorship is not as simple as we may assume when reading a letter from our grandmother or other loved one today. Hart quotes Morton on this point: "If an amanuensis gives us something quite unlike Paul, what right has anyone to call it Paul's?"[81] There is not much consensus on the matter, but looking at first-century writing practices, we can be sure that an amanuensis or other literary secretary was likely not just a simple transcriber of Paul's words, but an active participant in shaping letters, especially letters like Paul's, which are of such length and complexity that we cannot feasibly assume Paul to have dictated his every thought aloud to a poor transcriptionist.[82] It is more likely these letters went through multiple drafts, with coauthors and amanuenses contributing alongside Paul.[83]

Candida Moss adds much to this discussion with her recent article "The Secretary: Enslaved Workers, Stenography, and the Production of Early Christian Literature" (2023). Here, Moss discusses how enslaved workers and transcribers were seen and used in the ancient world, specifically in the formation of early Christian texts. Ancient authors frequently saw these workers not as agents in their own right, but as extensions of the author. As Moss describes somberly, "Descriptions of enslaved bodies portray them as tools, body parts, or prosthetic devices by which the wealthy liberated themselves from labour."[84] In correcting this idea of ancient secretaries, Moss writes, "Ancient secretaries drafted letters, corrected stylistic and grammatical mistakes, and improved manuscripts," to such an extent that we must consider authorship as "always collaborative."[85] Of course, the level to which these secretaries contributed is difficult—if

---

and Sosthenes and 16:21 possibly indicates usage of an amanuensis; Rom 1:1 and 16:22 indicates it was cowritten by Paul and Tertius (who probably served as an amanuensis). Lastly, Paul is sometimes listed on his own; see Gal 1:1, which identifies only Paul but 6:11 may indicate he had an amanuensis; Eph 1:1, 1 Tim 1:1, 2 Tim 1:1, and Titus 1:1 only list Paul as an author. That Timothy is meant as a coauthor here in Philemon seems relatively certain; see McKnight, *Letter to Philemon*, 53–54.

81. Morton quoted in Hart, *Prolegomenon*, 91.
82. Elmer, "I, Tertius" for a decent overview of the issue.
83. Elmer, "I, Tertius," 51–59.
84. Moss, "Secretary," 36.
85. Moss, "Secretary," 22.

not impossible—to gauge entirely, in no small part because ancient authors purposefully obscured both the agency of these figures and the level to which they intellectually contributed to a work's production.[86] Moss finds numerous instances, for example, of Roman authors who considered it a debasement of one's personal character to admit to having any intellectual influence from an enslaved or freed secretary or research assistant, to the point that even scribal errors or mistakes were chocked up more readily to the premature publication of an unready draft than the hand of an errant secretary;[87] simply admitting error on the part of one's secretary was more humiliating to the elite and slave-owning class than concocting a narrative of an unready draft being disseminated.

Perhaps the most notable issue discussed here pertaining to an amanuensis is the influence they have on the style and content of a given letter. As Hart says regarding vocabulary and stylistic analyses:

> Potential difficulties with this approach include that it does not account for the developments or variations in a single author's style, and does not allow for a situation involving the use of an amanuensis who writes in a style distinctive from the person giving instruction.[88]

Accordingly, I think that one potential method of accounting for this is to take inventory of coauthors and known amanuenses when analyzing styles and characteristics. For example, Philemon lists Paul and Timothy as coauthors. As such, while Paul may have a style distinctive from Timothy's, we also have several other letters purported to have been written by these two. Thus, we can compare the styles and vocabulary of those specific letters to get an idea of what is going on with Philemon. Here we can account for the multiplicity of authorship, since we have multiple examples of these authors writing together.

Establishing authorship is rather complex, and I wish to make it known that when I discuss pseudonymity and Paul's role as an author, I am specifically questioning if Paul had any direct involvement in producing the Letter to Philemon. In this volume, I question whether Paul's hand, voice, or agency was ever intentionally and directly employed to produce this text at all. I will then question whether coauthorship is present at all, or if this may in fact be an authenticating device used by pseudonymous

86. Moss, "Secretary," 36–40.
87. Moss, "Secretary," esp. 37–39.
88. Hart, *Prolegomenon*, 102.

works to manufacture a sense of legitimacy. For me to talk of Philemon as "authentic" or to talk of its "authenticity" in this volume is to talk of Philemon as the (at least partial) product of Paul's own free will, whether by dictating words, writing it himself, or contributing a notable portion to the work's composition. This excludes Philemon from being "authentically Pauline" if we were to, say, categorize it as a text written by copying from his letters but without his input or just with his signing off on the piece.[89] When we see authors copying from their predecessors, there is still, in a sense, a level of involvement from the predecessor, but if that predecessor had no direct agency in producing a newer text based on their work, we cannot conclude it is "authentic."

ORIENTING THIS VOLUME

To determine whether something is authentic, we need to answer a number of questions. Firstly, we start from the problematic basis that determining authenticity requires having a starting point, or (as Hart calls it) a "Pauline Archimedean point" of comparison.[90] My Archimedean point for this volume is not going to derive from mere assumption of the consensus. Instead, I will borrow rather heavily from the initial works of Van Manen and Eduard Verhoef, who have handled this subject in detail.

Verhoef, with similar reasoning to Van Manen, has proposed in multiple publications the following methodology for determining if a letter can be considered authentic in the broadest sense:[91] (1) We start with the letter containing the largest sample size, which gives us the largest possible breadth of an author's vocabulary, style, and theology as well as potential historical clues for who this individual purports to be. In this case, we start with Romans as our sample, as it is the largest of the works attributed to Paul. (2) We look at the prescript and derive "Paul" as our stand-in name for this author. This name is simply out of convenience, as we know of no

---

89. In short, it makes little sense to ascribe a letter to Paul that he had virtually no hand in writing, and only took credit for its production.

90. Hart, *Prolegomenon*, 105.

91. See Verhoef, "Determining the Authenticity of the Paulines," 83–86; "Willem Christiaan van Manen," 225; "Authenticity of the Paulines Should Not Be Assumed"; "Holländische Radikale Kritik," 431–32. For Van Manen and his dissertation, see Verhoef, "Willem Christiaan van Manen," passim.

other name to apply here.[92] When I speak of an authentic "Pauline" letter, I reference this character. (3) We consider the vocabulary, style, theology, and historical clues of the other letters and compare them, which allows us to assemble a general view of who authored what letter. (4) From this, we can assemble a general outline of who this figure is, what he believed, and how he wrote (or how he wrote in connection with other authors).

As noted above, a few of these points can be contentious. Starting with Romans is, of course, somewhat arbitrary; however, choosing the text with the largest sample size also provides us with the largest starting position (thus, the best chance of recognizing similarities and differences between many letters with more accuracy). Additionally, there is the issue of coauthorship, though I have already given a potential way to account for this (i.e., comparing letters claimed to be coauthored against each other and then against the Pauline texts which claim singular authorship). Verhoef contends that stylistic and vocabulary overlaps may also indicate potential borrowing from a forger.[93] As a result, caution is due at every step here. I would further add two points to Verhoef's model: (5) We then look for literary dependencies elsewhere, which aids us in determining a *terminus ad quem* for when this author was writing. Literary dependencies may also determine whether document X utilizes document Y and so provides a *terminus a quo* for X's composition (and potential hints of forgery practices).[94] (6) We assess known historical contexts for the traditional views on these documents. If traditional views fail to sufficiently adhere to the known historical data, then it increases the likelihood that said document may be a forgery practicing in anachronism. For this, we assess the internal data against the backdrop of what was generally known about similar and analogous situations in the ancient world (i.e. imprisonment, letter writing, etc.).

Turning to Romans, we get a broad overview of who this "Paul" is. Furthermore, because Romans is likely cited in *Didache* 5.2 (cf. Rom 12:9),

---

92. A few indefensible theories notwithstanding, see Hansen, "Evaluation of the Neo-Dutch Radical School."

93. Verhoef, "Determining the Authenticity of the Paulines," 85.

94. When determining literary dependency, there needs to be definite evidence of reliance that points only in one direction, i.e., X relies on Y. One piece of evidence showcased recently is editorial fatigue; see Goodacre, "Fatigue in the Synoptics." A more recent example of a modern forgery was discovered by Kipp Davis; see "Caves of Dispute," 260–61, where a forger utilized a critical edition of the Hebrew Bible and accidentally copied (editorial fatigue) a text apparatus mark from the critical edition onto the forged Dead Sea Scroll fragment.

Ignatius' *Letter to the Smyrnaeans* 1.1 (cf. Rom 1:3), and Polycarp's *Letter to the Philippians* 6.2, 10.1, 10.3 (cf. Rom 14:12, 12:10, and 2:24 respectively), we can be relatively certain that the Letter to the Romans was written prior to the second century.[95] Additionally, I would contend with a growing number of academics that the Gospel of Mark (written ca. 70–80 CE) and the Acts of the Apostles (90–120 CE) also cite Paul's letters, including Romans.[96] As such, I would propose that the *terminus ad quem* is at least 70 CE. One could provide an earlier *terminus ad quem* if one were to date 1 Clement earlier, though because it is frequently argued that 1 Clement may have some relationship to Romans, this gets problematic.[97] I find a second-century date for 1 Clement to be more likely, following Otto Zwierlein.[98]

With this, we can begin our investigation of other letters in the Pauline corpus. Verhoef comes to the general conclusion that "Paul" wrote or had a direct hand in writing (in addition to Romans) Philippians and 1 Thessalonians (in his essay "Determining the Authenticity of the Paulines") and 1 and 2 Corinthians (in "The Authenticity of the Paulines Should Not be Assumed").[99] I would further add Galatians, which I think fares well under similar analyses, though it is worth noting the few challengers to this claim over the years.[100] In these same works, Verhoef uses this meth-

---

95. It is worth mentioning that the letters of Ignatius have also faced some habitual scrutiny over authenticity, though this does not necessarily preclude their second-century dating; see Lookadoo, "Date and Authenticity of the Ignatian Letters." See also Detering, *Fabricated Paul*, 86–98; Van Manen, *Wave of Hypercriticism*, 74–85; Van den Bergh van Eysinga, *Oudste christelijke Geschriften*, 1:183–93.

96. Theophilos, "Roman Connection," 53–61 gives several reasons to consider Romans a potential source for Mark. See also Ferguson, *New Perspective* (which contends that Mark used at least Romans, 1 Corinthians, and Galatians); Dykstra, *Mark Canonizer of Paul*, esp. 69–91. For Luke-Acts, see Tyson, *Marcion and Luke-Acts*, 15–22.

97. For an early date, see Herron, *Clement and the Early Church of Rome*. See also, more recently, Bernier, *Rethinking the Dates of the New Testament*, 239–50. There is also a middle-date position that places 1 Clement in the late first century; see Knopf, *Commentary on the Didache and on 1–2 Clement*, 62–63.

98. Zwierlein, *Petrus in Rom*, 245–331. For compelling evidence of 1 Clement's reliance on Romans, see Downs, "Justification, Good Works, and Creation." Conversely, the Dutch Radicals argued that 1 Clement was inauthentic; see Detering, *Fabricated Paul*, 86–98. That said, inauthenticity does not imply late dating, so regardless of Detering (and company's) conclusions on the authenticity of 1 Clement, there is no reason to date it especially late.

99. Verhoef, "Determining the Authenticity," 91; "Authenticity of the Paulines," 150–51.

100. Aside from the Dutch Radicals, see O'Neill, *Recovery of Paul's Letter to the*

odology to argue that the the letters of Paul and Seneca and the Pastorals are not from the same hand as the others. Stylometric analyses have been done on each of these letters as well, generally confirming these results.[101] Notably, Philemon does not cohere with other epistles particularly well under a stylometric analysis; however, this should not necessarily be taken as proof of inauthenticity; the text has an exceptionally small sample size to work from, leading some academics to dismiss its stylometric analysis altogether.[102]

Under this framework proposed by Verhoef, my Archimedean point is Verhoef's results, which generally cohere with consensus positions.[103] In what follows, I will analyze the evidence for Philemon according to most of these criteria save theology, since I do not believe there to be enough content to make certain pronouncements on this topic in Philemon. Furthermore, I believe such a subject has the most caveats out of all of Verhoef's points, as Paul's theology and ideas clearly evolved over time, allowing for contradictions to arise (it is also partial to the intersubjective judgments of modern

---

Galatians, who challenges the authenticity of large portions of Galatians. Hoehner, "Did Paul Write Galatians?" notes that many of the methods used for assessing the inauthenticity of texts, if applied to Galatians, could arguably lead to the conclusion that Galatians was not authentic. Hoehner, of course, thinks that Galatians is authentic (169). For a more genuine attempt at arguing against Galatian's authenticity, see McGuire, "Did Paul Write Galatians?" Price, *Amazing Colossal Apostle,* 411 pushes the theory that Marcion penned the original letter to the Galatians based on a statement in Tertullian that Marcion had "discovered" the text (*Against Marcion* 4.3.2; note that Price also miswrites this as "5.3.1" and later miscites it as "4.3.1" on page 411). The claim is dubious and hinges on a poor conception of the Latin (and English, for that matter), as well as Tertullian's larger text. Firstly, we find that Tertullian has a separate version of Galatians and even finds discrepancies with Marcion's (*Against Marcion* books 4–5). In 4.3.2, Tertullian writes: *Sed enim Marcion nactus epistulam Pauli ad Galatas . . .* The relevant term *nactus* has a range of meanings in Latin. Deriving from *nanciscor,* it can also indicate "to stumble across" or simply "to find" in the sense of personal discovery, rather than having (as Price wishes it) discovered a never-before-seen original letter. Even in English translations, "discover" carries a semantic range. Price's entire thesis is bunk; his utilization of quotes from Marcion to reconstruct an original Galatians (and find endless swathes of interpolations) is futile and methodologically incoherent.

101. Savoy, "Authorship of Pauline Epistles Revisited."

102. Campbell, *Framing Paul,* 254–60; Beale, *Colossians and Philemon,* 439–42. Neumann, *Authenticity,* 124, who otherwise utilizes stylostatistical analysis, contends that Philemon is simply too small to even get a "cut" from.

103. One notable critique would be that privileging Romans could bias the results, to which this is readily accepted. However, when compared to 1 Clement and other texts, Romans arguably has the most authoritative claim to antiquity, further justifying this bias.

critics, myself included).[104] I will start by discussing the few points usually uttered in favor of Philemon's authenticity. Next, I will discuss the letter's literary contents and the numerous oddities present, which align it much closer to the other pseudonymous "prison epistles." After this, I will analyze the letter's style and vocabulary. I will lastly propose a potential schema as to why a letter of this kind may have been forged in Paul's name and when it could be plausibly dated. My proposal is that the evidence as it stands is, at best, inconclusive on Pauline authorship and potentially indicates that the letter is, in fact, not from the same "Paul" (or any of his usual scribes) who had a hand in writing Romans, 1 and 2 Corinthians, Philippians,[105] Galatians, and 1 Thessalonians. Instead, the letter may belong to the same corpus as Colossians (which I consider to be inauthentic) and easily functions as a commentary on certain passages within that text. While results cannot be entirely conclusive, in no small part due to the small size of the letter, I think that it is fair to say we have little reason to consider Philemon authentic. At the minimum, agnosticism is entirely justified.

This does not mean these arguments will necessarily be convincing, and in fact I fully expect that academics will rebut many of them. But, as I argue in my conclusion, if we contend that no arguments presented here demonstrate the inauthenticity of Philemon, then we must instead reevaluate how we have determined the inauthenticity of other epistles. If, for instance, stylistic and grammatical variations are deemed unremarkable or unconvincing in Philemon's case, then we ought to reevaluate why we view these methods as authoritative for epistles like 1 and 2 Timothy or Titus, which also have extremely small sample sizes. It is my contention, following Justin Paley, that the field proliferates double standards where Philemon is concerned, which this volume endeavors to expose. Merely claiming that arguments for inauthenticity are unconvincing does not itself demonstrate that authenticity is the correct view of Philemon; authenticity is not a null but is itself an assertion that requires argumentation and justification (see chapter 1). My ultimate goal with this book is not to prove that Philemon is a forgery, though I do believe the evidence tilts in favor of this conclusion. My true goal is getting scholars to engage in questions of authenticity more seriously and proactively, especially on texts that they have, until now, assumed to be authentic with virtually no coherent argumentation

104. Hart, *Prolegomenon*, 102, who notes this same pitfall.

105. Following Baur, I would also note my skepticism regarding the authenticity of Philippians as well, but this book is already too large without rambling on this subject.

in support. It is my view that the authenticity of Philemon has not been accepted for legitimate reasons and instead has more in common with a dogmatic belief than an informed, scholarly position.

I am, fundamentally, an amateur. I do not pretend that this will convince many scholars or bring down a consensus on the authenticity of Philemon. My only hope is that it prompts academics to think differently about how they have tackled the issue of authenticity (i.e., by not doing so at all regarding several of the seven generally accepted letters). If I can at least spark proactive thought and conversation on these matters, I will have achieved my goal.

1

The Case for Authenticity

As discussed in the introduction, the vast majority of scholars regard Philemon as being authentic, i.e., written by or under the auspices of the apostle Paul. I have not found a single commentary in German, English, French, or Dutch that asserts that the letter is inauthentic. Unfortunately, scholarly support for this text's authenticity most often comes in the form of a single brief paragraph nestled within a larger work. Finding any recent, comprehensive defenses of Philemon is extremely difficult, though some commentaries offer a few points worth discussing.[1]

In this brief chapter, I will address the works of Alford, Bruce, and Fitzmyer, who present the most noteworthy defenses from the last two-hundred years (the bar for "noteworthy" here being more than a single paragraph on the subject; see the introduction for a more detailed overview of the question's status in current scholarship). Meager as they are, these defenses provide some food for thought and, at the very least, illustrate what I and others (such as Paley, which will be discussed below) view as a double standard in methodology within Pauline studies of authorship. Some may wonder why I have chosen these samples, as the gaps between their publication dates span generations. The answer to this is simple: I am scraping the bottom of the barrel to find anything substantial enough to warrant a detailed response. In short, what I cover in this chapter represents the best I found during my extensive survey of the field.[2]

---

1. For a study devoted to this topic, see Hansen, "Authenticity of Philemon."

2. Some will opine with reference to Schenk's work, but this is largely addressed in

HENRY ALFORD

Henry Alford's defense of the authenticity of Philemon is one of the earliest, and certainly one of the most in-depth of the era. Even so, it remains unconvincing. He first begins with a discussion of Philemon's attestation by various church fathers (Origen, Tertullian, etc.) and an apologetic for the letter's complete absence from the works of Irenaeus and Clement of Alexandria.[3] His central thesis is that their unilateral declaration of Philemon's authenticity should inform our own decision in ascribing it to Paul's hand. Declaring it to be undoubted in ancient times (errantly, as he seems unaware of those early traditions which challenged it, as noted in this volume's introduction), Alford deems the issue basically settled.

The remainder of his discussion on the subject, however, is a sardonic dismissal of F. C. Baur's theories on Philemon. For Alford, there is no reason to imagine that a forger would create such a "simple" letter.[4] This complaint about Philemon is one that scholars readily employ even today, but objecting to it is as simple as observing a lack of imagination on the part of modern scholars and asserting that we should not ascribe a similar lack of imagination to a hypothetical ancient forger. Indeed, Baur himself, followed by Van Manen and others, eventually came up with quite a bit of circumstantial evidence for why Philemon may have been forged.[5]

One noteworthy caveat Alford introduces in his analysis is that the usage of *hapax legomena* and other stylistic oddities might indicate anything more than Paul's expansive vocabulary.[6] This is a reservation worth hearing, even in this present study; given the sample word size of the epistles and the frequency with which each letter showcases *hapax legomena* and other stylistic flourishes peculiar to said epistle, we could conclude that Philemon merely exhibits Paul's natural language variety. A counterpoint, though, is that if enough oddities compound, including ones that both

---

chapter 3. As a result, I do not discuss it in this chapter.

3. Alford, *Greek Testament*, 3:111–12.

4. Alford, *Greek Testament*, 3:112.

5. Baur, *Paul*, 305–8, who notes it provides practical commentary on Colossians and Ephesians; Steck, "Pliny im Neuen Testament," 570–84; Van Manen, *Wave of Hypercriticism*, 143–51, who combines Steck's and Baur's theses; Price, *Amazing Colossal Apostle*, 503–4, who follows Stephan Huller in arguing it was created to establish the authority of Onesimus; Schwab, *Echtheitskritische Untersuchungen zu den vier kleineren Paulusbriefen*, 152–56, argues for it being a forgery to support church authority. See more on these theories in chapter 4.

6. Alford, *Greek Testament*, 3:112.

internally and externally call into question the origins of the letter, then stylistic divergences become more noteworthy. As later chapters will demonstrate, Philemon potentially contains a myriad of stylistic oddities, ones that if seen in the Pastorals would give cause for doubt.

The rest of Alford's response can be summarized as chiding Baur with little thorough analysis of his argumentation; he regards Baur's work as self-"caricature,"[7] and he concludes that the univocal church tradition on Philemon's authorship topples Baur's arguments.

F. F. BRUCE

The next longest pertinent treatment of the issue that I found was F. F. Bruce's commentary on Philemon. He spends about two and a half pages discussing Philemon's authenticity,[8] for the most part summarizing portions of F. C. Baur and W. C. van Manen's opinions while having little in the way of original comment or content.

Most of what Bruce supplies can be categorized as polemical guff and dismissal. For instance, after summarizing Baur's views on Philemon's authenticity,[9] Bruce writes exactly nothing to refute what Baur offered; he dismisses his intellectual opponent with a wave of deafening silence before moving on to describe only a snippet of what Van Manen argued in his *Encyclopaedia Biblica* article from 1902.[10] Bruce takes particular aim at Van Manen's suggestion (following Rudolf Steck,[11] whom Bruce does not appear to have read) that Philemon was based on Pliny's letters to Sabinianus (*Ep.* 9.21, 24). Van Manen's reconstruction is characterized as "hypercritical and naïve," and "a farfetched explanation."[12] As is rather common among critics of the Dutch Radicals, Bruce denigrates Van Manen's ideas in lieu of arguing against them.

Notably, this is all Bruce has to offer in response to critics; he claims that, "on its face,"[13] the authenticity of Philemon is far more probable, yet he treats the claim as evidence of itself (elsewhere acknowledging that style

---

7. Alford, *Greek Testament*, 3:113.

8. Bruce, *Epistles to the Colossians, to Philemon, and Ephesians*, 191–93.

9. Bruce, *Epistles to the Colossians, to Philemon, and Ephesians*, 191–92.

10. Bruce, *Epistles to the Colossians, to Philemon, and Ephesians*, 192–93.

11. Steck, "Plinius im Neuen Testament," 570–84.

12. Bruce, *Epistles to the Colossians, to Philemon, and Ephesians*, 193.

13. Bruce, *Epistles to the Colossians, to Philemon, and Ephesians*, 193.

and language samples are too small to demonstrate authenticity[14]). What is notable about Bruce's response is not its merit or scholarly intrigue, but its naked display of indignation and offense at the thought of Philemon's inauthenticity, to the point that he forgets to offer evidence for his own theory. For Bruce, the mere presence of two uncompelling arguments for inauthenticity (which he cherry-picked and never considered in their entirety) is irrefutable proof that the only thesis worth considering is authenticity.

JOSEPH A. FITZMYER

Joseph A. Fitzmyer's commentary on Philemon presents little in terms of innovative discussion, though it remains one of the only to cite Van den Bergh van Eysinga's essay on the topic.[15] Fitzmyer contends:

> Today the authenticity of the Letter to Philemon is almost universally admitted, for there is no serious reason to question it. Moreover it is difficult to imagine why a pseudepigrapher of later date would want to concoct such a letter and pass it off as written by Paul of Tarsus. The language, vocabulary, style, and structure of the letter, as well as its argumentation, are notably Pauline.[16]

That most scholars accept the letter is, firstly, unsurprising and, secondly, immaterial. Fitzmyer, like many commentators, appeals to the majority even when the majority has largely failed to demonstrate their case. Alford, Bruce, and Fitzmyer represent the more comprehensive takes on the subject, and even still they contribute little. Fitzmyer asserts that the stylistic and linguistic conventions of the letter are all manifestly Pauline. This is a curious issue; as Campbell noted, by 2014 one required a sample size of around 500 words to compare a piece against an author's other writings and make reasonable determinations of authenticity.[17] Philemon barely totals 330 words, so how one can declare it "notably Pauline" is beyond me.[18] But

14. Bruce, *Epistles to the Colossians, to Philemon, and Ephesians*, 191.

15. Fitzmyer, *Letter to Philemon*, 73. Admittedly this is only in his general bibliography; he does not interact with the work at all.

16. Fitzmyer, *Letter to Philemon*, 8.

17. Campbell, *Framing Paul*, 259.

18. As Paley, "Questioning the Pauline Authorship of Philemon," 18 states aptly, "The letter to Philemon, at only 330 words, is the shortest text in the Pauline corpus and thus, objectively, a very small sample size for any kind of statistical analysis. As a result, it is often not included in such statistical studies."

even if we could make an accurate determination on such a small sample size, in following chapters I will demonstrate numerous peculiarities even there. What of this letter's "structure"? This too seems a dubious category, in no small part because the letter is structured more like a standard personal letter, atypical for Paul's generally accepted corpus. In fact, as will be noted in later chapters, Philemon looks remarkably like one written by Pliny the Younger (*Ep.* 9.21 with a continuation of the subject in *Ep.* 9.24).[19] We can point to several structural and mechanical peculiarities in this letter (its address to an individual, its primary interest in the topic of slavery, the more reserved language that "Paul" uses, etc.). Thus, as Knox wrote, "But the fact is that it [Philemon] is far from being an ordinary letter," and he continues, "A rather extensive search through papyri and other ancient letters has failed to disclose anything even remotely resembling it in form."[20] Structurally, it is unlike any of the unquestioned Pauline letters. The only other personal letters with which it shares some resemblance are the Pastorals, which even Campbell does not consider from Paul's hand.[21] Fitzymer at another point makes this note:

> In v 19 Paul speaks of writing "with my own hand." That may mean that he himself wrote the whole letter. It could also mean that at a certain point in his dictation to a scribe or amanuensis he snatched the pen and wrote a few words of that verse. That detail, however, cannot be utilized in the discussion about the authenticity of the Letter to Philemon as a whole, because that could be a literary device to make it sound authentic. The judgment about

19. Steck, "Plinius im Neuen Testament," 570–84 goes as far as to suggest that Pliny's letter was a possible model for Philemon (see also Van Manen, see Price, ed., *Wave of Hypercriticism*, 145–46, 149–50; and Van Manen, *Handleiding voor de Oudchristelijke Letterkunde*, 59; Price, *Amazing Colossal Apostle*, 503–4). Other scholars have long noted these similarities, though some try to put distance between the letters (i.e., Fitzmyer, *Letter to Philemon*, 20–23; Ip, *Socio-Rhetorical Interpretation*, 7–9; Knox, *Philemon Among the Letters of Paul*, 16–18). For instance, Seesengood claims that the freedman of Sabinianus is not a runaway, and that Paul never asks Philemon to forgive Onesimus while Pliny does so with the freedman (Seesengood, *Philemon*, 61–62).

20. Knox, *Philemon Among the Letters of Paul*, 51–52.

21. Campbell, *Framing Paul*, 392–403 suggests an anti-Marcionite origin for the letters, which I would agree with. Little does Campbell realize that Dutch Radicals had prototyped this argument earlier; see Price, *Pre-Nicene New Testament*, 640, 654–55 and *Amazing Colossal Apostle*, 505–30; Detering, *Fabricated Paul*, 106–55 (who sees a Marcionite background for much of the Pauline corpus). In contrast, only a handful of figures still cling to the Pastoral authenticity, e.g., Carter, *Pastoral Epistles*, 10.

the Paline [*sic*] authenticity of the letter does not depend on that
verse.[22]

This caveat is well worth making. As Crüsemann observes, this is potentially the case with 2 Thessalonians, which may be attempting to "suppress
the first letter [1 Thessalonians] by declaring it a forgery" through its assertion of authenticity from Paul's hand (2 Thess 3:17).[23] However, at this
juncture one simply wonders what the pro-Pauline authenticity position
really stands upon.

Has Fitzmyer made any noteworthy or pertinent points in defending this letter's authenticity? It seems not. Instead, Fitzmyer claims several
things that scholars have typically taken for granted, in no small part due to
a dearth of substantive investigation into Philemon.

DOUBLE STANDARDS WITH PHILEMON

A discussion of Philemon's authenticity is incomplete without a discussion
of double standards historically at play when verifying said authenticity.
Justin Paley recently published on this topic and indicted the ways most
academics have handled the authenticity of the Pastorals, all while neglect-
ing to mention that most of their same arguments and problems can likewise be directed at Philemon.[24]

For instance, (1) Barclay's commentary asserts that the familiarity of
various figures named to the letter writer is evidence of Pauline authorship.[25]
This would never be accepted as an argument in favor of the authenticity of
the Pastorals, though, which match up with the authentic epistles' naming
conventions just as well as Philemon or Colossians. In another case, (2)
scholars claim that style is a determiner for authenticity in the case of the
Pastorals (occasionally with Colossians and Ephesians as well) while ignoring striking stylistic peculiarities in Philemon (see chapter 3). Additionally,
(3) scholars often use narrative inconsistencies or problems to argue that
various letters cannot be harmonized as Pauline based on what we know
about Paul and the first century. Yet, as Paley notes, there is a strong case

22. Fitzmyer, *Letter to Philemon*, 8–9.

23. Crüsemann, *Pseudepigraphical Letters to the Thessalonians*, 248. Cf. Price, *Holy Fable*, 3:152.

24. Paley, "Questioning the Pauline Authorship of Philemon," 17–20.

25. Per Paley, "Questioning the Pauline Authorship of Philemon," 17–18.

to be made that Philemon also contains some of these oddities, such as portraying Onesimus as an unconverted slave in a Christian household, which previous studies have shown would be highly irregular.[26]

We see that several double standards abound in addressing Philemon's authenticity, which will be further validated as this study progresses. Paley is, in many ways, quite right. Arguments commonly used to disregard the Pastorals or Colossians (and/or Ephesians) could easily be turned against Philemon, but scholars have been reticent to do so. Many seem not to have realized that these arguments can be turned around to begin with. Instead, we see them assert blanketly that Philemon is authentic—no ifs, ands, or buts about it—and on the few occasions they bother offering more than a sentence dismissing the problem, they typically rely on faulty arguments outlined above.

The authenticity of Philemon has, up to this point, rested upon an un-justified consensus that relies on double standards to function. Aside from this, scholars have a handful of ready-made arguments that rarely bear weight upon closer inspection. That the arguments in favor of authenticity have been, up to this point, unconvincing is not itself evidence of inauthen-ticity (discussed below); it is evidence of scholars being all too comfortable with not accounting for some of their core beliefs regarding the Pauline epistles. They take authenticity for granted, assuming it without question, and they reiterate it with the same conviction as those old church fathers. This mindset needs correction.

AUTHENTICITY, A DEFAULT POSITION?

There is an apparent tendency to assume that arguments against a let-ter's authenticity being unconvincing or invalid means we can conclude authenticity by fiat. As seen above with the likes of Fitzmyer and Bruce, pro-authenticity cases largely come down to stating that inauthenticity is unlikely. More overtly, Douglas A. Campbell's approach is to assume a letter's authenticity until someone demonstrates its inauthenticity, i.e., an "innocent until proven guilty" presumption.[27] I believe that such a position is misguided and seeks to place the burden of proof only on those arguing against authenticity.

---

26. Paley, "Questioning the Pauline Authorship of Philemon," 19.

27. Campbell, *Framing Paul*, 25.

This effectively ignores that there is a more reasonable default position, which is to not assign a truth value in either direction: to conclude that the evidence of both sides (authenticity or inauthenticity) is insufficient or has not been established to conclude either direction. This is, essentially, a state of philosophical agnosticism on the question and is, arguably, the most reasonable default or null position to take, which is how Verhoef approaches the issue.

Firstly, arguing *against* an alternative hypothesis does not automatically make your own hypothesis probable. Say two people (A and B) are arguing over whether or not a deity (X) exists. A says yes, X does exist. B says no, X does not exist. Say they conclude that neither A nor B supply convincing arguments for their side. Is either's case strengthened by the other's being unconvincing? Not necessarily, because their own case remains unconvincing. Imagine an observer (C) comes on the scene and says that neither's argument is reliable or convincing, and we cannot assign a truth value to X's existence. Thus, we can only conclude that we cannot affirm either position as better than the other. In the case of Philemon, we could be stuck in a similar situation; it is not enough for scholar A to argue that B is unconvincing regarding authenticity. They must put forward a positive case that is *more* convincing than B's, otherwise C's position, agnosticism, is the most justified position. As Verhoef writes:

> Scholars who defend the inauthenticity of the Pastorals sum up a series of arguments that should support their opinion, whereas scholars who defend the authenticity of the same epistles constrain themselves to refuting these arguments. But even if these arguments can be invalidated, the authenticity is not yet proved.[28]

This is a valid position, but one completely ignored and overlooked by Campbell and others, who treat the question of authenticity as having only two answers (and in which Campbell privileges the claims of the positive camp). Given this, the most valid starting position is to make no presumption in either direction about the (in)authenticity of a particular letter. Its case must be arbitrated.

A problem that appears with Philemon is that evidence is scant and potentially consistent with both theories of inauthenticity and authenticity. This will be seen with the sample size problems and style but could also exist elsewhere. Say that in chapter 2, where I discuss narrative and literary

---

28. Verhoef, "Authenticity of the Paulines," 129.

problems with Philemon, another scholar argues that these issues are consistent on the side of pro-authenticity. In that case, they are consistent with both inauthenticity and authenticity. If we cannot decide between the two clearly, then the evidence cannot be determined in favor of any hypothesis, which again makes agnosticism the most justified null. If this keeps happening, and none of the evidence clearly favors any position, then neither inauthenticity nor authenticity can be affirmed.

In either outcome, the thesis of my book stands: Philemon's authenticity has been taken for granted. It is a widespread assumption that has been misbestowed upon much of the Pauline corpus (and especially upon Philemon), and we cannot keep treating authenticity as the de facto position from which to start every line of questioning.

2

Paul, Prison, Properties: Internal Literary Issues

It is worth commenting on the full contents of Philemon. In discussions of Philemon's authenticity, one will regularly happen upon the sentiment that it is hard to believe anyone would invent such a small and personal letter containing such mundane and general characteristics. F. F. Bruce, for example, provides one dry summary of the letter in contrast to Van Manen's own thesis that the letter was inauthentic:

> There is no need to propound such far-fetched explanations of a document which, in the judgement of most critics as of most general readers, bears a much more probable explanation on its face—namely, that is [*sic*, read "it"] is a genuine letter of Paul, concerning a slave called Onesimus, who somehow needs the apostle's help restoring good personal relations between him and his master, and that Paul quite naturally takes the opportunity at the beginning and end of the letter to send greetings to other members of the household.[1]

Is this really all there is to this letter? Is this all that bears discussion when it comes to the issue of its authenticity? Bruce's summation is, in my view, an obvious attempt to transform the letter into a more mundane sphere, something so general that it seems ridiculous "on its face" to make any arguments for its inauthenticity. This seems evidenced by the denouncements of such doubts and arguments for inauthenticity as

1. Bruce, *Paul*, 396.

"far-fetched explanations" and similar, which clearly relegates any doubter to a position of irrationality. They can be rejected, then, without further effort or comment.

In this chapter, my primary focus is the broader literary contents of Philemon and what makes it stand out. On the assumption that this epistle belongs to the "authentic" Pauline corpus (i.e., alongside Romans, 1 and 2 Corinthians, Galatians, Philippians, and 1 Thessalonians), Philemon's contents stand out, not only because it is a personal letter in form (unlike all other Pauline letters), but for its specific contents as well (topics, themes, even particular descriptions and mannerisms).

PAUL AND IMPRISONMENT

One of the most recognizable scenes from early Christian literature is that of a disheveled Paul writing a letter in his cell after having been captured and imprisoned by Roman guards. I can personally remember this scene being acted out at events like vacation Bible school, or my pastor giving the audience a lengthy sermon about the hard life of persecution that Paul and other early Christians led. This fascination is not without precedent; 1 Clement 5.6 identifies Paul as having been imprisoned seven times. Meanwhile, five of the letters that make up the New Testament identify Paul as being a prisoner or in chains (Philippians, Colossians, Ephesians, 2 Timothy, and Philemon). And then we have two other fabricated letters: 3 Corinthians and the apocryphal Letter to the Laodiceans, which also use this setting.[2]

Paul's imprisonment is a standardized feature of pseudonymous letters in his name; aside from Philippians (which I have my doubts about), no other authentic Pauline epistle portrays Paul as a prisoner, except the one currently under question. Notably, Philippians differs from all other letters in the pseudonymous corpus, both in style and content, and similarly differs from Philemon. I wish to note here the specific terminology used.

2. The most definitive recent treatment of this letter is Tite, *Apocryphal Epistle to the Laodiceans*. It is also possible there was a letter from Paul to the Macedonians. Clement of Alexandria, *Protreptikos* 9.87.19–21 refers to this letter and quotes a segment of it, the first half of which appears to mirror Philippians 4:5, while the second half is unique among the Pauline corpus. Immediately after this quote, Clement mentions that Paul was a prisoner for the sake of Christ, which may imply this letter too was styled as a prison letter. Both this and the authenticity of any such letter to the Macedonians is speculative at best, however, so I only briefly mention it here.

In Phlm 1, Paul is described as δέσμιος or "prisoner." This term appears nowhere in the authentic Pauline corpus, but it does appear in the inauthentic letters (Eph 3:1, 4:1; 2 Tim 1:8). Instead, Philippians (1:7, 1:13–14, and 1:17) speaks of Paul as being in chains (δεσμοῖς), which is reflected once in Col 4:18 as well. This manner of introducing himself in Philemon's opening differs from all other letter introductions. Usually, Paul asserts himself as an apostle or slave (ἀπόστολος or δοῦλος) of Jesus Christ, such as Phil 1:1. Nowhere in the letter of Philemon does Paul ever assert his status as an apostle. It is true that 1 Thessalonians does not open with Paul declaring himself any of these things either, though he does affirm that title in 1 Thess 2:6. Van Manen and others have found these titles particularly strange, given what we find elsewhere.[3]

I cannot stress the relevancy of this situation, as this title was, in fact, a source of consternation for later scribes copying and preserving Philemon. The Nestle-Aland *Novum Testamentum Graece* (twenty-eighth edition) in fact lists several alternative readings, including one manuscript that replaces δέσμιος with αποστολος, one that contains the combined αποστολος δεσμιος ("apostle prisoner"), and two that replace δέσμιος with δουλος.[4] The Vulgate may also reflect this discomfort with the title "prisoner" and instead renders Phlm 1 as *Paulus vinctus Christi Jesu* ("Paul, bound to Jesus Christ"), which is often rendered incorrectly as "prisoner" in English translations.[5] This odd title of "prisoner," which is attested nowhere else in

---

3. For Van Manen, see Price, ed., *Wave of Hypercriticism*, 148; Van den Bergh van Eysinga, *Littérature chrétienne primitive*, 140, who relates it to Colossians and Ephesians. See also Seesengood, *Philemon*, 81. McKnight, *Letter to Philemon*, 51–52 notes this peculiarity, but opines similarity to the description of Paul as a slave of Jesus in other letters. I find this unconvincing as a parallel, and it makes little sense why Paul would not utilize the more common term δοῦλος in this instance. This is undercut further by McKnight's appeal to the potential similarities between Paul and Onesimus. McKnight writes: "The term 'prisoner' also intentionally identifies Paul with the analogous marginal condition of Onesimus, who could well have experienced the humiliation of being shackled: one 'in bonds' in prison is far closer to the slave Onesimus than Philemon" (*Letter to Philemon*, 52). Of course, this parallel would be even closer if Paul called himself by one of his usual titles: δοῦλος. McKnight simply does not register this oddity, and the parallel he attempts to construct actually furthers my case for δέσμιος being uncharacteristic of Paul.

4. Nestle-Aland, *Novum Testamentum Graece*, 655 (critical apparatus).

5. My view is that this is a harmonization to make the Latin text cohere with the Greek when rendering it in English. I believe my rendering is accurate given that Phlm 23 (Vulgate) refers to Epaphras as *concaptivus* to denote the prisoner status, which indicates this is not the same sense being invoked in verse 1. My guess is that the Vulgate was rendered from a Greek manuscript reading either δουλος ("slave") or the previously

the Pauline corpus, then, was a source of much confusion and obfuscation (something unnecessary were Paul writing and addressing himself as he generally does in his other epistles).[6]

We need not, however, take this title as necessarily negative in early Christian literature—this need to correct it likely originates in a need to make Philemon cohere with Paul's general assertions of status in other letters (as noted above). As Van den Bergh van Eysinga pointed out, this title is not one designed to denigrate the apostle Paul, but to potentially showcase his martyrological status.[7] It is, in fact, the highest honor to be a prisoner for Christ, which is borne out by the expansive mythology regarding Paul's imprisonment.[8] It is, however, a title that does not cohere with Paul's general self-descriptions.

The issue of Paul addressing himself as prisoner and not as apostle or slave of Jesus Christ, as was typical, is in keeping with one commonality in Christian tradition: the association of Paul with imprisonment. Notably, pseudonymous letters and later Christian writings were quite infatuated with the idea of Paul suffering from frequent imprisonment, and it became a *type scene* for forged letters in his name.[9] I would challenge whether any

---

unattested δεσμοῖς (akin to Phil 1:7).

6. The only related term used is in Philippians (1:7; 1:13; 1:14; 1:16), where it speaks of Paul being in "bonds" (δεσμός) but never uses the title of "prisoner." This term does not denote imprisonment itself but the specific manner in which Paul is imprisoned, i.e., chained up. This can also be used to refer to the bonds of the enslaved, see Schellenberg, *Abject Joy*, 65.

7. Van den Bergh van Eysinga, "Paulus' Brief aan Philemon," 14 writes: "Ten onrechte hoort men wel uit dat δέσμιος een verregaande bescheidenheid van den Apostel, die pozettelijk zijn Apostel-titel verzwijgt uit innigheid. Integendeel, de gevangene van Jezus Christus is geen deerniswaardige figuur maar de martelaar-heilige, een kerkelijk hoogwaardigheidsbekleeder van den allereersten rang." Cf. Detering, *Paulusbriefe ohne Paulus?*, 334.

8. For more on this topic, see Moss, *Myth of Persecution*, passim.

9. For forged letters, see Col 4:3; Eph 3:1; 2 Tim 1:8; 3 Cor 1 (numbering according to M. R. James); apocryphal Epistle to the Laodiceans 6 (numbering according to Tite, *Apocryphal Epistle to the Laodiceans*, 126). Beyond this, Paul is mentioned in various Christian epistles and texts for his imprisonments. For instance, 1 Clement 5.5–6 mentions he was imprisoned "seven times"; Cyprian, *Epistle* 5.2 mentions his imprisonment as well. (Thanks to Ricky Brock Jr. for the Cyprian reference!) The imprisonment of Paul also appears to be part of Polycarp's background, *Letter to the Philippians* 9, which references the "sufferings" of the apostles and names Paul expressly. We are also aware of other letters that were fabricated depicting authors sending or receiving letters in prison, including a handful of Apollonius's letters (*Life of Apollonius* 4.46 [LCL 16] contains several supposed correspondences between Musonius Rufus and Apollonius of Tyana, likely

authentic Pauline epistle was written from prison (much less at Ephesus, the commonly assumed *sitz im leben* for Philemon[10]) at all. While Philippians has often been assumed to indicate that Paul is imprisoned and being guarded, I am not entirely convinced that this is not an extended metaphor for his self-described status as a slave of Jesus Christ in the first verse. Even assuming literal imprisonment to be the case, I still see little corroborative evidence for Philemon being possibly authentic; the letter may, for instance, be referring to a form of house arrest wherein he could still receive visitors freely.[11] On the other hand, Standhartinger has noted that the term πραιτώριον in Phil 1:13 does not actually refer to a prison; it is a Latin loanword indicating a place of judgment, akin to a courthouse.[12] In short, we have no authentic Pauline letter that is clearly and unquestionably written from the confines of a Roman prison. On the contrary, the idea that Paul is jailed and writing for a slave who found him strains credulity, to some extent. As Neutel and Smit note on Roman prison conditions:

> During their confinement, prisoners could be tortured and maltreated in different ways, both by guards and by their fellow prisoners. Torture, including forms of food deprivation, isolation and continuous enchainment was often used as a way to gain evidence and confessions, and to discover the involvement of other people in the criminal act. It was thus a common experience for those who were accused of a crime.[13]

---

all fabrications). It seems that fabricating prison letters was not uncommon.

10. There are numerous reasons to doubt the imprisonment at Ephesus ever took place; it is never mentioned in the Acts of the Apostles, and there appears to be no such indication in the letters themselves. While people often cite Eph 1:1, the phrase "in Ephesus" (ἐν Ἐφέσῳ) is inauthentic, absent from several early manuscripts. See Nestle-Aland, *Novum Testamentum Graece* (twenty-eighth edition), 590. In my view, there is no reason to accept the imprisonment at Ephesus as fact. Other ancient commentators believed the letter was written from prison in Rome.

11. Phil 1:13–14 implies that the "palace" and his fellow Christians have witnessed his chains in some fashion, and this proves he is in chains for Jesus Christ. This is to further (Phil 1:14) strengthen and instill confidence in Christians beyond. The implication, in my view (assuming this details imprisonment at all and is not just an expansion on the "slave" of Jesus Christ motif), is that Paul is under a form of house arrest but with freely coming and going visitors. In which case, it makes the lofty and exaggerated language of imprisonment here all the more interesting (i.e., Paul is fabricated or mythologizing his own imprisonment, a tradition seen frequently in Christian circles).

12. Standhartinger, "Letter from Prison as Hidden Transcript," 117.

13. Neutel and Smit, "Paul, Imprisonment and Crisis," 31.

While we do have some letters from prisoners of antiquity, writing and delivering them seems to have been a strained process. It should also be noted that most of those cited by Neutel and Smit (and Standhartinger) are written centuries removed from Paul's own imprisonment in the Roman Empire.[14] While Roman prisoners could indeed receive visitors, isolation was likely a normative means of punishment. It was claimed, for instance, that Socrates received visitors and wrote hymns while he was in prison.[15] Others claimed that a few playwrights wrote some of their works from the confines of a cell.[16] I am not inclined to believe all these literary accounts. For one thing, I would contend we cannot reasonably rely on any accounts of Socrates' followers entering the prison or having post-trial debates with their mentor as anything besides fictions or heavily fictionalized accounts (whose historical cores are arguably not worth trying to recover, assuming we could).[17] Writing from prison could also result in immediate execution, especially writings that indicted the ruling classes.[18]

The location itself was probably some dark and musty hole in the ground (literally), not remotely conducive to creating in-depth or careful writings. Moss describes ancient prisons as follows:

> What we know is that such confinement was far from comfortable. Roman prisoners, as recent archaeological research has shown, were largely subterranean. Most consisted of small underground chambers. Ephesus's weather rarely dips lower than forty degrees Fahrenheit in the winter, but the high humidity and blustery winds make it feel much colder. Paul's subterranean chamber would have been damp, moldy, and bitterly cold. Most of the time it would have been almost entirely dark, with the only natural light in the room entering through a small lunate opening close to the ceiling. . . . Given his situation, it's surprising that Paul managed to write letters to his churches, but we know that he did.[19]

---

14. Neutel and Smit, "Paul, Imprisonment and Crisis," 40. The same is also true of Standhartinger, "Letter from Prison as Hidden Transcript," 115–16. There seems to be a noticeable dearth of letters written within the first two centuries CE from prison cells.

15. Neutel and Smit, "Paul, Imprisonment and Crisis," 40; Standhartinger, "Letter from Prison as Hidden Transcript," 124.

16. Standhartinger, "Letter from Prison as Hidden Transcript," 124.

17. For more on the Socratic problem, see Dorion, "Rise and Fall of the Socratic Problem."

18. Standhartinger, "Letter from Prison as Hidden Transcript," 124.

19. Moss, *God's Ghostwriters*, 70–71.

In keeping with this dangerous and inhospitable environment, even in the case of Philippians, written from the praetorium, he still was speaking in euphemism. Standhartinger argues that he veils references to his fellow prisoners, to his compatriots, and even refers to himself euphemistically as in "chains."[20] At no point does he outright call himself a prisoner. If the cautious mediation of his language is what Paul would ordinarily do under dire circumstances, as in Philippians, then assuming he would plainly state his compatriots, those receiving his letter, and his status as a prisoner casts severe doubt on Philemon's composer being under the pressures of a prison cell.

As such, the picture of Onesimus, who is most likely an enslaved person,[21] finding Paul chained up in a prison cell and then obtaining his aid in writing a letter of recommendation and reconciliation involves either a combination of historical coincidences that played out perfectly in favor of this letter existing, or it being yet another link in the chain that is forging Pauline letters which use imprisonment as contextual motif. This is notable, as while it is true that some prisoners were allowed visitation to conduct business, Onesimus is not conducting anything for the affairs of Paul; this is an intercession on the behalf of a no-status slave. This makes the scenario less plausible. In Christian tradition, these types of writings supposedly produced from prison are more often inauthentic forgeries than not[22]; therefore Philemon's mere scenery might be ample cause for minimal suspicion.

Perhaps what most indicts the letter's scenery is one of the last statements Paul makes to Philemon; in verse 22, Paul asks Philemon to prepare a guest room for him so that he might stay with them soon. Were Paul imprisoned, and knowing what Roman prisons were generally like, how he expected to be freed and see Philemon so soon is a mystery. Again, it appears that Paul is less a prisoner than a pampered guest. This is at odds with

20. Standhartinger, "Letter from Prison as Hidden Transcript," 128–29.

21. Green, "Paul's Letter to Philemon"; and Paley, "Questioning the Pauline Authorship of Philemon," 12–13.

22. Of the seven known epistles claiming to be from Paul and written from prison, five are likely inauthentic in my estimation: Colossians, Ephesians, 2 Timothy, 3 Corinthians, Laodiceans. The other is Philippians which I am doubtful of, and the second is the one under consideration, Philemon. I am aware of only one other letter from the first two Christian centuries that is generally regarded as an authentic prison letter: Ignatius' *Letter to the Ephesians*. Notably, however, the Ignatian corpus has faced some challenges, see Detering, *Fabricated Paul*, 86–98; Killen, "Ignatian Epistles Entirely Spurious"; Lookadoo, "Date and Authenticity of the Ignatian Letters."

how Paul portrays prison in Philippians, where he is much more guarded and cautious. Either prison became much less severe in Ephesus (or Rome?) or this was not written from a prison.[23]

In actual prison letters surviving from antiquity, there is a much bleaker and desperate situation at play. Standhartinger, for instance, brings awareness to a letter from one Petakos to Zenon, who states, "Before you depart, please do not leave me behind in prison, for I lack the most essential things. I adjure you by the health of the father and siblings and the good of Apollonius. Farewell."[24] Letters from prison, along with diaries and similar, are consistent in their desperation and fear.[25] Philippians finds Paul contemplating a potential impending death sentence (1:18–26) and suffering from a lack of food and supplies in prison, which requires outside aid to remedy (4:10–19). And here, Paul is not writing Philippians from the prison itself, but the praetorium. Compare this to Phlm 22, which, by contrast, imagines Paul going to Philemon's house soon. These two letters do not cohere, and in fact Philemon's depiction of Paul in prison is so surface level and (at first glance) superfluous that Hausrath considered all such references to be potential interpolations (akin to Colossians).[26]

Were we to regard the prisoner motif as being simply that, a motif, then we can begin to see the literary device's utility to prospective forgers. In Philemon, the primary function of Paul's imprisonment could have been to place him in a similar context to Onesimus, thus creating a more compelling case on the enslaved man's behalf. Phlm 10 relays that Onesimus' conversion occurred while the "authority" figure of Paul was in chains, making them both people whose freedoms have been restricted and constrained. Likewise, Onesimus' mobility as a slave absent his master is seen as useful for Paul, whose mobility was neutralized via bondage (Phlm 13). These are the only times that Paul's imprisonment is brought up (save to mention that Epaphras is also imprisoned; see Phlm 23), and it

23. Which only makes sense if the letter were forged, since the author of Philemon clearly wants the imprisonment imagery to be literal, see Beale, *Colossians and Philemon*, 376 for discussion.

24. Standhartinger, "Letter from Prison as Hidden Transcript," 116.

25. Standhartinger, "Letter from Prison as Hidden Transcript," 116–17 notes other such examples. For instance, the martyr Perpetua lamented, "I was terrified, as I had never before been in such a dark hole. What a difficult time it was! With the crowd the heat was stifling, then there were the many informers of the soldiers" ("Letter from Prison as Hidden Transcript," 116).

26. Hausrath, *History of the New Testament Times*, 122–23.

is to liken himself to Onesimus and instill the figure with utility; as Paul is imprisoned, he wishes for Onesimus to take up a mantel of mission work. This grants the slave authority, mirroring both Paul's teaching in 1 Cor 7 (see below for further evidence of letter copying) that all are slaves in Christ and his later reception of Onesimus as a beloved brother (parallel Col 4:9). All of this is to say, imprisonment does not seem to be something Paul undergoes in Philemon—it is literary, as opposed to literal. Unlike in Philippians, there are no references to the locale (1:13), preparation in case of death (1:20–21), having a secondary individual come to care for Paul and provide him necessities like food (2:25), or being sent materials for aid (4:18). This imprisonment serves more to promote Onesimus rather than convey anything tangible about Paul's setting, which is consistent with forgery. This likewise explains the relative looseness of references to Paul's imprisonment in Colossians and Ephesians; if we take Philippians as our authentic standard, following Verhoef, these other three (Philemon, Colossians, Ephesians) seem to be at odds with the former and with what we should generally expect from Roman prisons.

SLAVERY, CONVERSION, AND SLAVE CONVERSIONS

One other noticeable problem is that the historical backdrop of Onesimus' conversion is not likely. As Paley writes in his paper on Philemon's authenticity:

> In the case of Philemon, apart from the ambiguity around the location and circumstances of Paul's imprisonment, there is another element of the epistle that is quite odd based off what we know about the first century world. Namely, the fact that Onesimus was not a believer while his master, Philemon, was. In his study on slave conversion in early Christianity, Taylor states the point plainly: "If Onesimus were the nonChristian slave of a Christian slave-owner, in the sense of being in no way connected with the church to which his owner belonged, he would seem to have been an exception to general custom in the church of the first century." While it is true that we are working with very limited evidence, as we have few accounts of slave conversion in early Christianity, especially in the first and early second centuries, this would seem to go against other ancient evidence we have which shows that,

when the *paterfamilias* "converted" to a new belief system, the rest of the household followed suit.[27]

As I will discuss in chapter 4, this is yet another issue better explained by the letter being a forgery unconcerned with historical accuracy; as contentions about slavery likely germinated in the second century CE, a byproduct of that milieu could have been newfound interest in master-slave dynamics and Onesimus' conversion.

Regardless, this too provides a narrative issue with the text; not only does Paul hardly look imprisoned, but the slave conversion narrative seems equally muddled.[28] One might argue that Onesimus is not being converted; however, the language that "Paul" uses is difficult to explain any other way.[29] The paternalistic phrasing seems to imply that Onesimus has come into the family of Christ under Paul while he was in prison and separated from the rest of Philemon's household, which would incur the historical implausibility that Paley notes. Combined with the incoherent way Philemon handles Paul's supposed imprisonment, we are less certain that this refers to historical events.

Tangentially, we may question this narrative if baptism is implied; how had Onesimus been brought into the family of Christ under Paul when Paul sits in a prison cell unable to baptize? Bianchini has argued rather convincingly that historical baptisms were often conducted as part of a public manifestation of one's faith and a desire to participate in resurrection the dead in Christ.[30] Paul attests in 1 Cor 1:10–17 that baptism was exceptionally important in nascent Christian communities, to the extent that baptized Christians considered who baptized them to be something of a status symbol, which in some cases caused dissent among ranks (and consternation

---

27. Paley, "Questioning the Pauline Authorship of Philemon," 19.

28. Counter explanations that this is not a conversion seem less likely. Green, "Paul's Letter to Philemon" makes a solid case that this probably deals with a runaway and new convert.

29. Crossley, *Why Christianity Happened*, 162–63 (following Nicholas Taylor) argues that Onesimus may have been "converted" against his will but never attained any "Christian" conviction. Fleeing the household meant Onesimus was severed from the family and church, so it became necessary to complete the conversion experience with Paul in prison. This argument seems exceptionally convoluted and steeped in numerous problematic assumptions. What do we mean by "Christian" in this sense? What if Onesimus is not a runaway (a common counter as there is no clear evidence of this in the letter)? Callahan, *Embassy of Onesimus* argues against the runaway slave interpretation entirely.

30. Bianchini, "Crux Interpretum of 1 Cor 15:29."

for Paul). Considering Paul remarks that he quite literally lies in chains in a prison, the idea that he conducted a baptism seems untenable. This case is strengthened if we consider that Paul likely monetized his baptisms, as was typical for other ritual acts of the time.[31] So where did Onesimus get the money, and why would we assume that a prisoner of Rome is simply conducting ritual business as usual? Of course, this all depends on whether Paul's language indeed indicates baptism. If so, it creates tensions in the text's narrative, as Mary Ann Beavis has pointed out.[32] If baptism is not of consequence here, then the issue vanishes, though many commentators do hold to the baptism image.[33] It is certainly plausible that the passage hints at baptism; therefore this stands as another narrative tension within the piece (if only tentatively).

PAUL AND LETTER COPYING

There are four letters supposedly written by Paul from prison that serve as the core "prison epistles" (Colossians, Ephesians, Philemon, and Philippians). In my opinion, all four of them are suspicious, specifically regarding their use of each other and other literary sources. The notion that Paul has a plethora of cowriters and letter carriers coming back and forth from prisons, or (further) that he makes spare copies of these letters to refer back to later is questionable. I will expand on clear cases of literary overlap in the following chapter, but I will go over some prime examples here (similar wording underlined):

Philemon	Colossians
1 Παῦλος δέσμιος Χριστοῦ Ἰησοῦ καὶ Τιμόθεος ὁ ἀδελφὸς Φιλήμονι τῷ ἀγαπητῷ καὶ συνεργῷ ἡμῶν	1:1 Παῦλος ἀπόστολος Χριστοῦ Ἰησοῦ διὰ θελήματος θεοῦ καὶ Τιμόθεος ὁ ἀδελφὸς

31. Bell, "Cost of Baptism?"

32. Beavis, *First Christian Slave*, 42–43.

33. Williams, "'No Longer a Slave'", 25; Byron, "Epistle to Philemon," 209; Glancy, *Slavery as a Moral Problem*, 32; Osiek, *Philippians and Philemon*, 139; Fitzmyer, *Letter to Philemon*, 108–9. Barth and Blanke, *Letter to Philemon*, 335 take issue with this assumption, however. Ancient Christians also interpreted the text in this way, see Ambrosiaster in Bray, *Commentaries on Galatians–Philemon*, 162; and Theodoret of Cyrus in Hill, *Commentary on the Letters of St. Paul*, 261.

3 χάρις ὑμῖν καὶ εἰρήνη ἀπὸ θεοῦ πατρὸς ἡμῶν καὶ κυρίου Ἰησοῦ Χριστοῦ	1:2 τοῖς ἐν Κολοσσαῖς ἁγίοις καὶ πιστοῖς ἀδελφοῖς ἐν Χριστῷ χάρις ὑμῖν καὶ εἰρήνη ἀπὸ θεοῦ πατρὸς ἡμῶν
4 Εὐχαριστῶ τῷ θεῷ μου πάντοτε μνείαν σου ποιούμενος ἐπὶ τῶν προσευχῶν μου	1:3 Εὐχαριστοῦμεν τῷ θεῷ πατρὶ τοῦ κυρίου ἡμῶν Ἰησοῦ Χριστοῦ πάντοτε περὶ ὑμῶν προσευχόμενοι
5 ἀκούων σου τὴν ἀγάπην καὶ τὴν πίστιν ἣν ἔχεις πρὸς τὸν κύριον Ἰησοῦν καὶ εἰς πάντας τοὺς ἁγίους	1:4 ἀκούσαντες τὴν πίστιν ὑμῶν ἐν Χριστῷ Ἰησοῦ καὶ τὴν ἀγάπην ἣν ἔχετε εἰς πάντας τοὺς ἁγίους

Did Paul happen to have a copy of 1 Corinthians or Colossians in prison while writing Philemon? Did he have Philemon around while writing those other two? To say nothing of Philippians, which shares an entire verse with Philemon word for word (see Phlm 25 and Phil 4:23). As I note in the next chapter, there is strong linguistic overlap with 1 Corinthians as well, making it fairly evident that whoever composed Philemon at least had access to 1 Corinthians.

That Ephesians is aware of Colossians has been long recognized, and the copying from Colossians makes many scholars wary of its authenticity.[34] The evidence points to Colossians and Philemon having a close relationship; Campbell even notes that it is hard to see why Philemon would have been canonized were it not linked to Colossians, given how many people apparently wished to omit it over a perceived lack of utility (discussed in chapter 4).[35] Furthermore, Colossians is likely aware of and utilizes 1 and 2 Corinthians elsewhere. From my view, the evidence is fairly secure: Philemon–Colossians seem to utilize previous letters and copy from them, contra Campbell.[36]

Given the precarious nature of letter writing from prison, the idea that Paul has a copy of 1 Corinthians on hand and can make several letters all apparently copying each other (and 1 Corinthians) begins to strain the imagination. In all the annals of ancient Greco-Roman letter writing, I do not think we have an analogue to this sort of literature copying or parallel

34. Ehrman, *Forgery and Counterforgery*, 182–90.

35. Campbell, *Framing Paul*, 259–60.

36. Campbell, *Framing Paul*, 286–92, 335 notes that stylometric analyses and such have been questionable and inconsistent regarding Colossians and Ephesians, but it is also worth noting that the studies he cites are fairly antiquated. Recent studies with more up-to-date methodologies since (and including) Ledger and Mealand (cited by Campbell) place the two in the non-Pauline correspondences, see Savoy, "Authorship of the Pauline Epistles Reconsidered."

wording occurring among any *authentic* prison letters. While Campbell avers that Paul may have kept copies of his letters and that they circulated in other congregations, his only evidence of this is Colossians (which, if inauthentic, may have been composed at a later date when copies were made and spread to other congregations, in which case it is not convincing evidence of what Campbell claims).[37] Again, in an environment where one could be executed, tortured, and spied on while writing letters, the idea that one could have retained copies of their previous literature is suspect and incredible. Far more likely would it be that Paul's letters would have been stripped from him upon imprisonment, traced by the Romans to find any "co-conspirators" that Paul may have had, and used to imprison them as well. One could also aver (as Campbell does in a footnote[38]) that Paul might have memorized his letters, but this again is based on the assumption that he kept copies, for which I find no convincing evidence to support.[39] Bernier likewise raised problems with Campbell's Pauline chronology—particularly methodological—which seem to make it untenable.[40] If authentic, I doubt there is a cogent way to order these letters chronologically.

The other explanation is that Colossians and 1 Corinthians copy from Philemon. This seems unlikely, at least as far as 1 Corinthians is concerned. This letter has little interest in anything to do with slavery, shows few thematic overlaps that point to Philemonic priority, does not copy the names of the various personalities, etc. But despite this, Philemon shows various overlaps in other places (see above). While 1 Corinthians contains a lot

37. Campbell, *Framing Paul*, 284.

38. Campbell, *Framing Paul*, 284n32.

39. Richards, "Codex and the Early Collection of Paul's Letters" suggests that Paul would have and that this was common practice among ancient letter writers. Contra Richards, we have many reasons to challenge this. Firstly, Paul is a missionary on the move, traveling between locations where he easily could have lost his letters (say to . . . a shipwreck, Acts 27–28; or imprisonment Phil 1:13). That he was able to produce multiple copies of the same letter in prison, from which epistles like Colossians or Philemon may have relied upon, is also rather ludicrous. While there is debate about how expensive papyrus was (Williams, "Textuality and the Dead Sea Scrolls," 77–78), some indications show a roll could be anywhere from one to three days wages depending on location (Mastnjak, *Before the Scrolls*, 30). Certain cost saving measures could be taken with papyrus, though, specifically opisthographic papyrus manuscripts (Williams, "Textuality and the Dead Sea Scrolls," 77–78). Given that in similar situations Paul opined being financially due to imprisonment (Phil 4:10–19), the idea that he can afford and purchase extra papyrus to pen personal copies of his letters seems strange from a material and economic perspective alone.

40. Bernier, "When Paul Met Sergius."

of theological material and so would be a prime candidate for Philemon to draw relevant terminology from, the same cannot be said vice versa, as Philemon has a clear and miniscule focus by comparison.

I will argue that (following Schwab[41]) Philemon appears to copy from Colossians for various linguistic reasons. In terms of narrative, we have some reason for considering Philemon to be post-Colossians. The portrayals of Onesimus are inconsistent, so Philemon must either take place chronologically before Colossians (in which case we wonder how Onesimus ends up back with Paul and why Epaphras is not also mentioned as a prisoner in Col 4:12; additionally, it creates confusion as to why Onesimus would be mentioned in Colossians, but not Philemon), at the same time as Colossians (the trip he takes back with Tychicus is the one where Onesimus delivers Paul's letter to Philemon), or just after Colossians is composed (which better accounts for Epaphras only first being mentioned a prisoner in Philemon 23; cf. Col 4:12). In this case, Onesimus arrives to see Paul, does a few errands while Paul figures out what to say, and returns to collect a letter addressed to his owner, Philemon. As James D. G. Dunn contended, it is far easier to see these letters composed at the same time or with Philemon composed *after* Colossians, not the other way around.[42] What further indicates that Philemon probably relies on Colossians is that Col 2:1 states that Paul had never met any of the church in Colossae. It appears that Philemon has Paul with several friends listed in verse 2,[43] and given that Philemon and Colossians are written by the same hand, it is hard to justify Philemon as being set anywhere but Colossae.[44] If Colossians relied upon

41. Schwab, *Echtheitskritische Untersuchungen zu den vier kleineren Paulusbriefen*, 136–56 provides much more evidence of Philemon being reliant on Colossians in sprawling and useful tables denoting all parallel language more comprehensively than I could ever hope to present here.

42. Dunn, *Epistles to the Colossians and to Philemon*, 37–38.

43. Price, *Amazing Colossal Apostle*, 503.

44. That Philemon is associated with Colossae appears to be a widely adopted consensus based on the mention of Archippus in Phlm 2 (cf. Col 4:17) and Onesimus in Col 4:9 as being one of the Colossians; see Campbell, *Framing Paul*, 261–68; Wall, *Colossians & Philemon*, 195–96, who suggests the Archippus from Col is the same in Philemon; Thompson and Longenecker, *Philippians and Philemon*, 160–61; Tamez, Kitteredge, Colombo, Batten, *Philippians, Colossians, Philemon*, 236–37; Hamm, *Philippians, Colossians, Philemon*, 27; Alan Thompson, *Colossians and Philemon*, 216–18; Patzia, *Ephesians, Colossians, Philemon*, 105; Verhoef, *Filippenzen, Filemon*, 97; O'Brien, *Colossians, Philemon*, 273; Pao, *Colossians & Philemon*, 342; Beale, *Colossians and Philemon*, 370; Fitzmyer, *Letter to Philemon*, 12–13, 88; McKnight, *Letter to Philemon*, 37; Bruce, *Epistles to the Colossians, to Philemon, and Ephesians*, 191. Balabanski, "Where Is Philemon?" has

Philemon, then this verse is inexplicable; due to Philemon's small size, this detail would literally be right in front of the author of Colossians. It is much easier to imagine Philemon's author missing a passage this size within a much larger work. If both letters were authentic, then they could not have been written close together, or Philemon could not have lived in Colossae.

Implying that Philemon has a dependency on Colossians is also its existence in the canon itself. Luke Timothy Johnson has recently argued that scholars (like Petersen and Wright) have spent no time arguing for the authenticity of Philemon. Instead, "if it is authentic, they seem to imply, then its place in the canon follows naturally."[45] He opines, "They spend no time puzzling over the odd fact that such a short note, written to an obscure personage in an unknown location, should have been preserved at all, much less included in the Pauline corpus with letters like Romans and Galatians."[46] Johnson argues, rather convincingly, that Philemon shares numerous rhetorical and thematic overlaps with Colossians and Ephesians, and that these overlaps were probably the reason it was brought into the canon.[47] While Johnson regards Philemon as authentic, the arguments he offers are just as applicable on the hypothesis of inauthenticity, i.e., that the similarities and rhetorical overlaps between these three are due to all of them being inauthentic and having intertextual relationships with each other. Despite his complaint that Philemon's authenticity is not argued for, Johnson himself assumes it and does not contend with its potential inauthenticity in any detail.

Thus, the letters being written by the same person with Philemon chronologically afterward makes the most sense of both letters' narratives and internal overlaps. In which case, Paul apparently has a large letter writing industry operating out of his prison cell.

Dependency, of course, does not itself determine inauthenticity unless one can demonstrate a reason why such dependence would be unlikely if authentic.[48] Campbell's suggestion is that Colossians was not fabricated but instead could have been based on copies that Paul kept of his letters.[49] His counterargument is specious, in my view; his parallel to 2 Thessalonians is

---

failed to convince me of an alternative.

45. Johnson, *Constructing Paul*, 248.
46. Johnson, *Constructing Paul*, 248.
47. Johnson, *Constructing Paul*, 249–71.
48. Campbell, *Framing Paul*, 284.
49. Campbell, *Framing Paul*, 284.

not particularly relevant, since they both have different stated contexts. In Colossians, Paul is supposedly writing from prison, unlike 2 Thessalonians. The idea that Paul managed to keep copies of 1 Corinthians, Galatians, and other letters stowed away in a prison cell which he could then copy is both ludicrous and potentially based on faulty argumentation.

While many ancient authors did keep copies of their letters, this was not a universal practice. Colossians 4:16, which Campbell cites, indicates that a single copy of Colossians and a letter to the Laodiceans[50] (now lost) would be passed around multiple congregations (which I find is in tension with Campbell's point that Paul kept and/or distributed multiple copies). Furthermore, assuming Paul possessed copies of his previous letters, it is far from likely that he was allowed to keep them upon imprisonment.[51] It is not the "mere fact of dependence"[52] that is suspicious, but the fact that it occurs in the context Colossians was supposedly written in, which Campbell and others do not address. As far as I am aware, we do not have any authentic writings from prison cells which display such outward signs of dependency on previous letters (probably because it was unfeasible). One of Campbell's other arguments is self-defeating considering other arguments he makes. Throughout *Framing Paul*, Campbell is skeptical of using style or similar elements as a basis for determining authenticity or authorship, yet he appeals to pre-Pauline creeds and hymns to explain away data which indicates Colossians relies on previous Pauline letters.[53] However, the only way to accurately identify these as pre-Pauline "hymns" or "confessions" (as Campbell labels them) is by their stylistic variation from the rest of Paul's writing. As such, Campbell's own critiques arguably disqualify his counterargument about Colossians.[54] Additionally, Leppä's

50. There is no evidence multiple copies of this letter were in circulation. Laodicea was a mere seventeen kilometers from Colossae, certainly close enough (literal walking distance) that the single copy could have been passed around and shared, which seems implied by "Paul's" command to do so with this single copy of Colossians.

51. As noted above, the expenses involving letter production make the idea that Paul was producing multiple copies while in prison fairly unlikely, and the idea that these copies would not have been confiscated seems unjustified.

52. Campbell, *Framing Paul*, 284.

53. Campbell, *Framing Paul*, 285–86.

54. Contra Campbell, I would critique the idea that these can be described as feasibly pre-Pauline for other reasons. For starters, we know it was certainly not beyond ancient writers to fabricate sources and traditions for their own purposes, and we see this even in New Testament writings; see Walsh, *Origins of Early Christian Literature*. In one case, we know that Paul at least tampered with the tradition quoted in 1 Cor 15:3–8 likely adding

work shows that Colossians likely knew about most of the Pauline corpus (including in combinations that are simply not compatible with Campbell's chronology).[55] Campbell's arguments against 2 Corinthians have little bearing on the clear dependencies between Colossians and 1 Corinthians, Romans, Galatians, 1 Thessalonians, Philippians, and possibly the Gospel of Mark, which Leppä shows with numerous tables.

In short, we should consider literary dependency (discussed more in chapter 3) to be far more significant in this case, as Philemon and Colossians are both written in the context of imprisonment. Notably, assuming Colossians are authentic (following Campbell), my contentions against Philemon here are sustained throughout this volume because I argue that Philemon is written *post-Colossians* anyway. To counteract this, it would have to be demonstrated that Colossians is both authentic and reliant upon Philemon.[56]

Excurses: Philemon and Philippians?

Thomas L. Brodie suggests (though perhaps not as in depth as one would wish) that Philemon's contents are actually modeled on Philippians, not Colossians. This would align partially, as we do find some noteworthy verbal correspondence (noted in the chapter below). Brodie writes:

> The letter to Philemon seems supremely occasional but it has a curious relationship to other epistles, especially Philippians, and particularly to the hymn on self-giving or self-emptying (Phil

---

in v.8 and either completely inserting or tampering with verse 6. That these are pre-Pauline simply cannot be taken at face value, as Campbell does. One must either demonstrate they are non-Pauline linguistically or find a manuscript of them independent from Paul's letters. Otherwise, we have reason to suspect Paul was creative enough to invent them. Thus, Campbell either has to admit the efficacy of stylistic concerns regarding the hymns (thus, his arguments contra Colossians' inauthenticity based on style hold little weight), or that these cannot be declared pre-Pauline (in which case, his arguments contra Colossians' dependency on the other epistles carries no weight).

55. Leppä, *Making of Colossians*, 225–55.

56. Though this also does not guarantee authenticity as I have described above. Philemon still could have been written in Paul's name and without his involvement, perhaps just on his behalf by a friend, and then he could have incorporated part of it.

2.1–13). Paul's sending of the beloved Onesimus is like a giving of his own body ("he is my heart," Phlm 12), and the change of status from slave to beloved brother is like the exaltation of Onesimus (Phlm 15–16). What happened to Christ is being applied to a specific life.[57]

Most will not be convinced enough by these "parallels" to see an intertextual relationship between Philemon and Philippians. However, Philemon's ending being verbally identical to Philippians and no other epistle (though a few are close) gives some reason to view this read as potentially credible.

STRUCTURAL INCONSISTENCIES

The Epistle to Philemon betrays numerous structurally atypical moves for a supposedly genuine Pauline letter. One that potentially displays a non-Pauline origin is "Paul's" insistence that he wrote it with his own hand (v. 19). While Paul does occasionally make similar claims, they almost always occur in the ending salutations rather than before, as they do in Philemon.[58] Other structural elements seem atypical of Paul's general letter constructing habits, but before too much is written about them, it is worth noting that we are dealing here with an atypical letter. As a personal letter, for which we have no other authentic Pauline examples, we would necessarily expect structural dissimilarities. Additionally, some would instead argue that the letter has more Pauline structural similarities in that it is a letter following the general formula: introductory greeting, blessing, argument, and closing salutations.[59]

PROBLEMS WITH ACTS

One last observation to be made is Philemon's potential inconsistency with Acts and Pauline chronology as a whole. It is generally accepted that the epistle was written to people in Colossae due to the close correspondences with Colossians, but some issues result from this read. Firstly, as Eurell writes, "With respect to Colossians and Philemon, we must admit

57. Brodie, *Birthing of the New Testament*, 586.

58. 1 Cor 16:21; Gal 6:11. This was pointed out online by Dr. Nick Elder (who argues that Paul himself wrote Philemon) and will be a point of discussion in his forthcoming paper, "'This Hand Is Validation,'" being published in *New Testament Studies*.

59. Beale, *Colossians and Philemon*, 375.

that Colossae is not mentioned in Acts, nor are the names Philemon and Onesimus."[60] In fact, no early church leader seems to have any idea that Paul was near or associated with Colossae until fairly late into the second century, and resolving these sources seems to necessitate a second imprisonment of Paul.[61]

Because of this, Evanson concluded that Philemon is inauthentic.[62] This might be too drastic in and of itself, depending on how much stock one puts in Acts as a source of Paul's life. The more one insists on the historical accuracy of Acts, the more its silence on any mission to Colossae becomes an issue. This becomes an even bigger problem when one reads early church fathers and finds a startling lack of any Pauline presence in that place until the letters to the Colossians and to Philemon first emerge in Christian texts. The lack of reference to a church of Colossae until much later into the second century (see chapter 4) again lends credence to the notion that this was a late development, not one that existed during the time Luke-Acts was first composed. We will revisit this in chapter 4.

CONCLUDING REMARKS

In summary, the internal elements of Philemon evince a lack of sincerity in the setting. The letter wants us to believe that it is Paul writing from prison, but when comparing it to the only widely accepted prison letter (Philippians) and records of ancient imprisonment standards, this becomes a stretch. Paul seems to allude to and quote his previous letters (how or where he kept copies in a prison is a mystery), and, unlike in Philippians, Paul is free and unfettered enough by his apparent imprisonment in Philemon to name co-conspirators, mention friends, and act as if he will be walking down to Philemon's house soon enough. While the setting of imprisonment does have utility, both to liken Paul to Onesimus and to grant Onesimus some responsibility (or authority) via their similar conditions, an appropriate

60. Eurell, "Second Imprisonment of Paul," 234.

61. Eurell, "Second Imprisonment of Paul" seeks to overcome this by positing that (A) Colossians/Philemon presuppose Paul had not visited Colossae yet, and (B) Acts may have known of these letters and chronologically placed them during the Roman imprisonment, but that Paul had not visited Colossae until *after* the Roman imprisonment. While this might work for Colossians, which presumes a lack of friends in Colossae, this does not work for Philemon, where the titular character owes his conversion to Paul (v. 19). In this case, Philemon necessitates Paul's proximity to Colossae.

62. Evanson, *Dissonance*, 320.

sense of urgency and the debilitating circumstances of prison seem lost on whoever authored this letter. Any noted similarities between the conditions and authority of Paul and Onesimus could just as easily provide a potential motive for forgery (see chapter 4).

3

The Language of Pseudonymity

THE CLAIM THAT PHILEMON fits general characteristics of Paul's style and vocabulary is occasionally used to justify its authenticity. For instance, Stuhlmacher reacts to F. C. Baur's criticisms with the following:

> In the meantime, exegetes have come to regard Philemon authentic because the form, style, and choice of words point to a genuine Pauline letter and the peculiar expressions (already noted by F. C. Baur) can be clarified due to the specific situation of the letter.[1]

Such comments, I believe, are not particularly informed on this issue. This is no surprise, as most critics have spent very little time analyzing Philemon's language and determining whether it aligns with the general characteristics of other commonly accepted Pauline epistles. Scholars only sometimes characterize Philemon's style as an oddity; like Seesengood, who writes:

> Though the voice of Philemon is generally consistent with the other six so-called undisputed letters of Paul, Philemon contains a substantial number of words used only once in these Pauline letters and in the New Testament. While Paul's characteristic love of wordplay or punning is present, the grammar, vocabulary, and style of Philemon deviate from the undisputed letters *more than*

---

1. Stuhlmacher, *Brief an Philemon*, 19–20 translation mine. See German: "Inzwischen hat die Exegese gelernt, den Phlm als authentisch zu betrachten, weil Form, Stil und Wortwahl auf einen genuinen Paulusbrief weisen und sich die schon von F. Chr. Baur notierten Besonderheiten des Ausdrucks aus der spziellen Situation des Briefes aufhellen lassen."

the Pastoral letters do. If one examines the grammar and vocabulary very closely, they seem idiosyncratic to and different from the Paul we know from his other letters. This would suggest concern regarding Philemon's authorship.[2]

Meanwhile, stylometric analysis places Philemon outside the confines of the other generally accepted epistles (though we should take this with a grain of salt, as the sample size for Philemon is small).[3] Thus, this assertion by Stuhlmacher and others is meritless. In this chapter, I will expand upon numerous peculiarities throughout Philemon, then critique what I perceive to be a double standard persistent throughout NT studies; if one is to take the Pastorals as inauthentic on the basis of vocabulary and style, they have every reason to do so with Philemon.

THE UNITY OF PHILEMON

While the unity of the received text of Philemon is virtually unquestioned today,[4] this has not always been the case. Indeed, there is perhaps precedent for reconsidering the stability of the text's present form, which complicates any picture of authenticity.

Heinrich Holtzmann, Adolf Hausrath, and Wilhelm Brückner infamously suggested there were major interpolations into an authentic text of Philemon.[5] As with those suggesting the whole letter is fabricated, Holtzmann's thesis was not met with positive reception; other scholars typically lumped him in with critics like Baur and dismissed him similarly.[6] Hausrath is rarely ever even mentioned. On the basis of several overlaps with Colossians, Holtzmann and Hausrath proposed that large portions of Philemon were glossed by later interpolators. Despite a chilly reception, their theory is not completely devoid of merit. At the very least, there is contradiction among early church leaders over the text's stability; while Tertullian (*Against Marcion* 5.21) asserts that Philemon escaped Marcion's

2. Seesengood, *Philemon*, 80, emphasis original.

3. Savoy, "Authorship of Pauline Epistles Revisited."

4. To date, I could find no major commentary that suggests noteworthy or significant interpolations, save the alterations from "prisoner" to "apostle" and such (see chapter 2).

5. Holtzmann,"Brief an den Philemon"; Hausrath, *History of the New Testament Times*, 122–23; Brückner, *Chronologische Reihenfolge*, 200–203.

6. E.g., Knox, *Philemon Among the Letters of Paul*, 28.

editing hand by virtue of its brevity, Epiphanius (*Panarion* 42.12.1) declares that he will not quote from Marcion's edition because the letter had been altered. BeDuhn cautions that we should put no weight on Epiphanius' claim;[7] however, this judgement may be too hasty. Given scant evidence of Philemon from the first three centuries, we can only wonder what its initial contents looked like. For example, Tertullian and Marcion could have received shorter identical versions of the epistle, but over time the letter was exaggerated with interpolations that Epiphanius (writing more than a century after the fact) regarded as authentic and that now form the basis of our *textus receptus*.[8]

Hausrath observes that Philemon's opening verses also bear striking similarity to Colossians, perhaps suggesting an editor (assuming Philemon contains an authentic core). Further, the Epistle to Philemon's superfluous usages of prison imagery may "recall the manner in which the interpolator of the Epistle to the Colossians makes his Paul clank his chains every now and again."[9] To think claims of interpolation baseless is perhaps too far. Additionally, we do not typically associate the elaborate preamble in verse 4–6 with personal letters.[10] Removing these passages (see the appendix) makes the remaining passage flow rather well.

However, another hypothesis accounts for these problems while maintaining the epistle's general integrity: Philemon was written *after* and *based on* Colossians. This does not necessarily imply that Philemon is inauthentic, though, coupled with observations in chapter 2 and chapter 4 (as well as the dubious status of Colossians among Paul's letters), it certainly adds to our suspicions. For the most part, though, this theory does account for the issues raised by Holtzmann, Hausrath, and Brückner. Were Philemon based on Colossians (as I will argue below), then the elaborate introduction is a textual leftover. This would also explain why the letter is both sent to a single man, Philemon, and a collective. So, for the remainder of this book, I will presume the unity of Philemon.[11]

7. BeDuhn, *First New Testament*, 225.

8. It certainly would not be the first time the *textus receptus* had preserved lengthy interpolations (cf. Mark 16:9–20).

9. Hausrath, *History of the New Testament Times*, 122. Cf. Brückner, *Chronologische Reihenfolge*, 200–203.

10. Cf. 1 Tim 1:1–2 and 2 Tim 1:1–2.

11. Reading Philemon without the supposed interpolations also opens several possibilities, and as such I have rendered a version (see appendix) without the proposed glosses for those wishing to ponder that potentiality.

GRAMMATICAL AND VOCABULARY VARIATIONS

This section is brief for several reasons. Firstly, style has recently come under fire as a poor metric for determining authenticity in the Pauline epistles; numerous contextual circumstances can alter a person's style, and many conditions could create comorbidities. For instance, Paul claims to be elderly in Philemon (v. 9); he claims to be a prisoner (v. 1); he may have a coauthor (v. 1, though v. 19 contradicts this); the genre of the letter is different (it is not a community theological treatise, but a personal letter of recommendation), etc. Each of these factors can radically alter a person's style; therefore many of the following points could be considered insignificant. As such, while I will list them, the weight of my textual arguments does not hinge upon them, save to point out when the letter deviates from what is typically considered Pauline.

Most of these come down to inflections and conjugations that are not always present in the six other commonly accepted letters. Some variations are unique to Philemon,[12] while others occur only in the disputed epistles.[13] Similarly, there are a few words that only appear in Philemon,[14] or are only shared with the disputed epistles,[15] alongside a few phrases.[16] Some only appear in the commonly accepted epistles, and one can certainly argue for

12. Phlm 1 συνεργῷ; Phlm 7 ἀδελφέ (cf. Phlm 20) and ἔσχον; Phlm 8 ἀνῆκον (cf. ἀνῆκεν Eph 5:14 and Col 3:18, per Van den Bergh van Eysinga, "Paulus' Brief aan Philemon," 12); Phlm 9 πρεσβύτης (cf. Eph 6:20; Tit 2:2); Phlm 12 κατέχειν and διακονῇ; Phlm 14 γνώμης, ἠθέλησα, and ἑκούσιον; Phlm 15 ἐχωρίσθη and ἀπέχῃς; Phlm 19 προσοφείλεις; Phlm 20 ἀνάπαυσόν; Phlm 21 ποιήσεις; Phlm 22 ἑτοίμαζέ, ξενίαν, and χαρισθήσομαι.

13. Phlm 7, 8 πολλὴν (cf. Eph 2:4; 1 Tim 3:13); Phlm 8 παρρησίαν (cf. Eph 3:12, 6:19; Col 2:15; 1 Tim 3:13); Phlm 11 εὔχρηστον (cf. 2 Tim 2:21); Phlm 18 ἠδίκησέν (cf. Col 3:25); Phlm 21 εἰδὼς (cf. 1 Tim 1:9; 2 Tim 2:23 and 3:14; Titus 3:11); Phlm 23 συναιχμάλωτός (cf. Col 4:10).

14. Phlm 8 ἐπιτάσσω; Phlm 11 ἄχρηστος; Phlm 12 ἀναπέμπω; Phlm 19 ἀποτίνω; Phlm 20 ὀνίνημι; Phlm 22 ξενία. The proper names Φιλήμων (v. 1) and Ἀπφία (v. 2) are only found in Philemon.

15. Phlm 1, 9 δέσμιος (cf. Eph 3:1, 4:1; 2 Tim 1:8); Phlm 11 εὔχρηστος (cf. Tim 2:21, 4:11). The other proper names (not Paul or Timothy) are shared with the disputed epistles, see Ἄρχιππος, (cf. Col 4:17), Ὀνήσιμος (cf. Col 4:9), Ἐπαφρᾶς (cf. Col 1:7, 4:12), Μᾶρκος (cf. Col 4:10; 2 Tim 4:11), Ἀρίσταρχος (cf. Col 4:10), Δημᾶς (cf. Col 4:14; 2 Tim 4:10), Λουκᾶς (cf. Col 4:14; 2 Tim 4:11).

16. Phlm 17 εἰ οὖν (cf. Col 3:1). Phlm 21 construction εἰδὼς ὅτι is unique. Thanks to Mark Bilby for pointing this out.

Philemon's style evoking Paul's in other places.[17] One element that becomes clear from this textual analysis is the proliferation of genitives in Philemon, which is characteristic of Colossians but not of the typically accepted Pauline epistles. By my count, 53 words of Philemon's total 335 are inflected in the genitive, totaling 15.82 percent of the entire epistle.

Notably—and I must mark this as a major caveat—much of this language that does not appear in the authentic Paulines comes down to the specific grammatical forms we are seeing. Many of these terms appear in different grammatical forms across the authentic Paulines; however, we still come away with numerous terms that are either unique to Philemon or shared only between Philemon and either deutero-Pauline or non-Pauline texts. Additionally, while the numerous genitives are a noteworthy comparison to Colossians,[18] we ought be cautious in drawing solid conclusions from this. Style is a notoriously difficult tool to approximate authorship, and one could also easily emphasize similarities in style between Philemon and the other commonly accepted six.[19]

PATCHWORK LETTER: COPYING THE PAULINE CORPUS

The most noteworthy evidence against Philemon's authenticity is its apparent reliance on other Pauline epistles. Philemon was likely one of the later letters written (certainly so, if inauthentic), specifically post-*Hauptbriefe*.[20] Notably, Philemon is a key point among scholars arguing that Colossians and Ephesians are, too, authentic, due to the (as seen below) numerous similarities between Philemon and Colossians. Yet, since they have not established Philemon's authenticity, any argument based on it for the authenticity of Colossians-Ephesians is, on its face, faulty. The close relationship between Philemon, Colossians, and Ephesians cannot be brushed aside here.[21]

17. Brookins, *Ancient Rhetoric and the Style of Paul's Letters*.

18. Ehrman, *Forgery and Counterforgery*, 176.

19. Brookins, *Ancient Rhetoric and the Style of Paul's Letters*.

20. Bernier, *Rethinking the Dates of the New Testament*, 181.

21. Seesengood, *Philemon*, 81; Pao, *Colossians & Philemon*, 22–23 and several others have commented on this relationship. Many commentaries group Philemon, Colossians, and Ephesians together due to their overlaps, which demand they be treated as parts of the same body of work, either with an authentic letter being copied (usually Philemon is upheld as authentic) or with all three being authentic. Debates on whether Colossians or Ephesians is authentic are ongoing, as Pao notes (*Colossians & Philemon*, 22), but it is

Conversely, I think that Philemon's relationship to other epistles, especially taking larger portions together, likely points to Philemon being constructed by a scribe who had the other epistles right in front of him. This scenario seems entirely unlikely for Paul; the idea that Paul, sitting in a crowded, dirty, inhumane prison filled with hungry and angry men more than willing to rat him out, could simply unroll his previous epistles and consult them (and Timothy) while drafting a private letter to his friend strains credulity. This leaves us with another option: someone else constructed Philemon by utilizing portions of Paul's other letters. This would explain numerous issues, including the resemblances that Philemon bares both to other generally accepted letters and to the inauthentic letters. By far the most detailed and recent analysis of this issue has been Günther Schwab's dissertation, entitled *Echtheitskritische Untersuchungen zu den vier kleineren Paulusbriefen*.[22] Schwab's full work includes large tables demonstrating Philemon's relationship with Colossians in immaculate detail; I suggest readers peruse his volume, as I can only provide a few pieces of his evidence in my own.

The first indicators of reliance are a few verses that could also determine the directionality of some copying. Regardless of assumptions on authenticity, it is generally accepted that Philemon was written after the *Hauptbriefe*, as we find references to some of those texts. Phlm 3 (χάρις ὑμῖν καὶ εἰρήνη ἀπὸ θεοῦ πατρὸς ἡμῶν καὶ κυρίου Ἰησοῦ Χριστοῦ) is found verbatim in authentic and inauthentic letters, among other close parallels.[23] My view is that either Colossians or 1 Corinthians is the origin for Philemon's verse, since other passages show a close relationship between Philemon and Colossians (with Ephesians likely being parasitic on Colossians[24]). Phlm

---

quite possible to view Colossians and Ephesians as being from the same author.

22. Schwab, *Echtheitskritische Untersuchungen zu den vier kleineren Paulusbriefen*, 136–56.

23. McKnight, *Letter to Philemon*, 60 also lists 2 Thess 1:2; 1 Cor 1:3; 2 Cor 1:2; Phil 1:2; and Titus 1:4 See also A. Thompson, *Colossians and Philemon*, 218; Patzia, *Ephesians, Colossians, Philemon*, 107; Fitzmyer, *Letter to Philemon*, 90–91; Pao, *Colossians & Philemon*, 366; Detering, *Paulusbriefe ohne Paulus?*, 335; Van den Bergh van Eysinga, "Paulus' Brief aan Philemon," 12, among several others. Van Manen (Price, ed.), *Wave of Hypercriticism*, 148) contends it could have originated with any of the epistles.

24. Ehrman, *Forgery and Counterforgery*, 183–85 notes many points on this matter, including a case where Ephesians appears to copy an entire twenty-nine words from Colossians in sequence, which itself would indicate plagiarism or copying in virtually any other piece of literature. In modern disciplines, we would consider this clear evidence of plagiarism.

1 has δέσμιος Χριστοῦ Ἰησοῦ, which, as noted before, only appears in Eph 3:1 and 4:1. The ending of Phlm 2 (καὶ τῇ κατ' οἶκόν σου ἐκκλησίᾳ) is very similar to Col 4:15 and 1 Cor 16:19.[25]

While it has been proposed that the first verses of Philemon are based on Ephesians and 1 Corinthians, it is likely that Colossians is the origin.[26] For comparison, I have reconstructed the following table as found in Schwab's volume (similar wording underlined):[27]

Philemon	Colossians
1 Παῦλος δέσμιος Χριστοῦ Ἰησοῦ καὶ Τιμόθεος ὁ ἀδελφὸς Φιλήμονι τῷ ἀγαπητῷ καὶ συνεργῷ ἡμῶν	1:1 Παῦλος ἀπόστολος Χριστοῦ Ἰησοῦ διὰ θελήματος θεοῦ καὶ Τιμόθεος ὁ ἀδελφὸς
3 χάρις ὑμῖν καὶ εἰρήνη ἀπὸ θεοῦ πατρὸς ἡμῶν καὶ κυρίου Ἰησοῦ Χριστοῦ [cf. Col 1:3]	1:2 τοῖς ἐν Κολοσσαῖς ἁγίοις καὶ πιστοῖς ἀδελφοῖς ἐν Χριστῷ χάρις ὑμῖν καὶ εἰρήνη ἀπὸ θεοῦ πατρὸς ἡμῶν
4 Εὐχαριστῶ τῷ θεῷ μου πάντοτε μνείαν σου ποιούμενος ἐπὶ τῶν προσευχῶν μου	1:3 Εὐχαριστοῦμεν τῷ θεῷ πατρὶ τοῦ κυρίου ἡμῶν Ἰησοῦ Χριστοῦ [cf. Phlm 2] πάντοτε περὶ ὑμῶν προσευχόμενοι
5 ἀκούων σου τὴν ἀγάπην καὶ τὴν πίστιν ἣν ἔχεις πρὸς τὸν κύριον Ἰησοῦν καὶ εἰς πάντας τοὺς ἁγίους	1:4 ἀκούσαντες τὴν πίστιν ὑμῶν ἐν Χριστῷ Ἰησοῦ καὶ τὴν ἀγάπην ἣν ἔχετε εἰς πάντας τοὺς ἁγίους

These are not remotely the only instances of comingling between Philemon and Colossians that Schwab points out.[28] Outi Leppä further demonstrates others:[29]

25. This similarity is noted in Detering, *Paulusbriefe ohne Paulus?*, 335; Van Manen, *Wave of Hypercriticism*, 148; Van den Bergh van Eysinga, "Paulus' Brief aan Philemon," 11. This likely refers to a house used for meetings of Christians; see Fitzmyer, *Letter to Philemon*, 89.

26. Detering, *Paulusbriefe ohne Paulus?*, 335; Van den Bergh van Eysinga, "Paulus' Brief aan Philemon," 12.

27. Schwab, *Echtheitskritische Untersuchungen zu den vier kleineren Paulusbriefen*, 136–37. See also Reuter, *Synopse zu den Briefen des Neuen Testaments*, 48–225.

28. Schwab, *Echtheitskritische Untersuchungen zu den vier kleineren Paulusbriefen*, 151–52 for a useful table comparing the following: Phlm 1 and Col 1:1; Phlm 2 and Col 4:17; Phlm 3 and Col 1:2; Phlm 4 and Col 1:3; Phlm 5 and Col 1:4; Phlm 5 and Col 1:8–9; Phlm 6 and Col 1:9–10; Phlm 7 and Col 1:12; Phlm 8 and Col 3:18 (and 3:22–4:1 at large); Phlm 9 and Col 1:23–24, 4:18; Phlm 10, 16 and Col 4:9; Phlm 19 and Col 4:18; Phlm 23–24 and Col 4.10–14. The continuity between the two is, in my opinion, undeniable.

29. Leppä, *Making of Colossians*, 225. For another thorough treatment of the synoptic relationship between Colossians and Philemon, see Reuter, *Synopse zu den Briefen des*

Philemon	Colossians
8 Διό πολλὴν ἐν Χριστῷ παρρησίαν ἔχων <u>ἐπιτάσσειν</u> σοι <u>τὸ ἀνῆκον</u>	3:18 Αἱ γυναῖκες <u>ὑποτάσσεσθε</u> τοῖς ἀνδράσιν ὡς <u>ἀνῆκεν ἐν</u> κυρίῳ[30]
[...] 10 ὃν ἐγέννησα ἐν <u>τοῖς δεσμοῖς</u> Ὀνήσιμον [...] 12 <u>ὃν ἀνέπεμψά</u> σοι [...] 13 ἐν <u>τοῖς δεσμοῖς</u> τοῦ εὐαγγελίου	4:8 <u>ὃν ἔπεμψα</u> πρὸς ὑμᾶς [...] 4:9 σὺν Ὀνησίμῳ [...] 4:18 μνημονεύετέ μου <u>τῶν δεσμῶν</u>

If we propose that Philemon is based on Colossians, its relationship to 1 Corinthians seems surer, as Colossians itself appears to borrow from the Corinthian correspondence (4:18, cf. 1 Cor 16:21 have verbatim language ὁ ἀσπασμὸς τῇ ἐμῇ χειρὶ παύλου in reference to Paul writing the ending greeting[31]). However, more concrete is that Philemon's language overlaps with 1 Corinthians in numerous places. The table below shows these parallels underlined:[32]

Philemon	1 Corinthians
19 ἐγὼ <u>Παῦλος</u> ἔγραψα <u>τῇ ἐμῇ χειρί</u>, ἐγὼ ἀποτίσω ἵνα μὴ λέγω σοι ὅτι καὶ σεαυτόν μοι προσοφείλεις	16:21 Ὁ <u>ἀσπασμὸς τῇ ἐμῇ χειρὶ Παύλου</u>.
16 οὐκέτι ὡς δοῦλον ἀλλὰ ὑπὲρ δοῦλον, <u>ἀδελφὸν ἀγαπητόν</u> μάλιστα ἐμοί, πόσῳ δὲ μᾶλλον σοὶ καὶ ἐν σαρκὶ καὶ <u>ἐν κυρίῳ</u>. [...] 20 ναί <u>ἀδελφέ</u> ἐγώ σου ὀναίμην <u>ἐν κυρίῳ</u> ἀνάπαυσόν μου τὰ σπλάγχνα ἐν Χριστῷ.	15:58 <u>Ὥστε ἀδελφοί</u> μου <u>ἀγαπητοί</u> ἑδραῖοι γίνεσθε ἀμετακίνητοι περισσεύοντες ἐν τῷ ἔργῳ τοῦ κυρίου πάντοτε, εἰδότες ὅτι ὁ κόπος ὑμῶν οὐκ ἔστιν κενὸς <u>ἐν κυρίῳ</u>
20 ναί, ἀδελφέ, ἐγώ σου ὀναίμην ἐν κυρίῳ <u>ἀνάπαυσόν μου</u> τὰ σπλάγχνα ἐν Χριστῷ	16:18 <u>ἀνέπαυσαν γὰρ τὸ ἐμὸν</u> πνεῦμα καὶ τὸ ὑμῶν ἐπιγινώσκετε οὖν τοὺς τοιούτους

Neuen Testaments, 49, 51, 53, 55, 61, 65, 95, 99, 189, 205, 209, 211, 213, 215, 217, 219, 221, 223, 225.

30. Note that Christ and "Lord" are often interchangeable, thus the difference of Χριστῷ/κυρίῳ is insignificant. It arguably draws the passages further into alignment.

31. For more advanced overlaps, see Schwab, *Echtheitskritische Untersuchungen zu den vier kleineren Paulusbriefen*, 103–4. Leppä, *Making of Colossians*, 224–55 demonstrates that Colossians likely had knowledge of most of the authentic Pauline corpus (including 1 Corinthians). See also Price, *Amazing Colossal Apostle*, 469–81 who argues for several close relations to 1 Corinthians. Additionally, see Brookins, *Ancient Rhetoric and the Style of Paul's Letters*, passim for various comparisons.

32. Schwab, *Echtheitskritische Untersuchungen zu den vier kleineren Paulusbriefen*, 128.

21 πεποιθὼς τῇ ὑπακοῇ σου ἔγραψά σοι <u>εἰδὼς</u> <u>ὅτι</u> καὶ ὑπὲρ ἃ λέγω ποιήσεις	15:58 Ὥστε <u>ἀδελφοί μου ἀγαπητοί</u> ἑδραῖοι γίνεσθε ἀμετακίνητοι, περισσεύοντες ἐν τῷ ἔργῳ τοῦ κυρίου πάντοτε <u>εἰδότες</u> <u>ὅτι</u> ὁ κόπος ὑμῶν οὐκ ἔστιν κενὸς ἐν κυρίῳ
2 καὶ Ἀπφίᾳ τῇ ἀδελφῇ καὶ Ἀρχίππῳ τῷ συστρατιώτῃ ἡμῶν καὶ <u>τῇ</u> <u>κατ᾽</u> <u>οἶκόν</u> <u>σου</u> <u>ἐκκλησίᾳ</u> [...] 23 <u>Ἀσπάζεταί</u> <u>σε</u> Ἐπαφρᾶς ὁ συναιχμάλωτός μου ἐν Χριστῷ Ἰησοῦ	16:19 <u>Ἀσπάζονται</u> <u>ὑμᾶς</u> αἱ <u>ἐκκλησίαι</u> τῆς Ἀσίας. <u>ἀσπάζεται</u> <u>ὑμᾶς</u> ἐν κυρίῳ πολλὰ Ἀκύλας καὶ Πρίσκα σὺν <u>τῇ</u> <u>κατ᾽</u> <u>οἶκον</u> <u>αὐτῶν</u> <u>ἐκκλησίᾳ</u>

The proliferation of terms shared between 1 Corinthians and Philemon is similarly unignorable.[33] Of particular note is that a number of these terms cluster around chapter 7 of 1 Corinthians, where Paul briefly remarks on slavery.

Another argument in favor of Philemon utilizing Colossians is that these verses of Philemon seem spliced together; it is easier to imagine Philemon altering previous texts for its own purposes than it is to imagine other authors dropping snippets of Philemon into their own works, especially as Philemon's brevity leads to a dearth of content useful to Colossians and others. Critics may reply that Paul means to address the congregation with greetings in verse 3 while in verses 4–5 he means to address Philemon alone, but why would he not simply refer back to the subject? The letter seems confused as to whom it is addressed, as it remains largely in singular until verse 22, when Paul again calls on a plurality to prepare a guest room for him. Is this letter addressed to the whole household, the congregation, Onesimus and Philemon, Philemon and Apphia, Philemon alone, everyone? This speaks to a writer confused as to whether they are drafting a personal letter or congregational one, thus intermixing them.

More elements point to Philemon's potential reliance on the authentic Pauline corpus. Phlm 16 (οὐκέτι ὡς δοῦλον) immediately calls to mind Gal 4:7 (οὐκέτι εἶ δοῦλος), alongside other portions. Take the mirroring language of "brother" in Phlm 16 (ἀδελφὸν) and "son" in Gal 4:7 (υἱός): in both there is a declaration of kinship and commonality between slave and master, unified through God (θεοῦ in Gal 4:7; κυρίῳ in Phlm 16). The phrase "beloved brother" (in Phlm as ἀδελφὸν ἀγαπητόν) in various forms appears

---

33. For instance: ἑτοιμάζω (1 Cor 2:9, cf. Phlm 22); ἐλπίζω (1 Cor 16:7, cf. Phlm 22); ὀφείλει (1 Cor 7:36, 9:10, 11:7, 11:10, cf. Phlm 18); χωρίζω (1 Cor 7:10, 7:11, 7:15, cf. Phlm 15); ἀνάγκην (1 Cor 7:26, 7:37, cf. Phlm 14); ἐμαυτὸν (1 Cor 4:3, 4:6, 7:7, 9:19, cf. Phlm 13); παράκλησιν (1 Cor 14:3, cf. Phlm 7); ἐνεργής (1 Cor 16:9, cf. Phlm 6); κοινωνία (1 Cor 9:5, 10:16, cf. Phlm 6).

in Eph 6:21 (ἀγαπητὸς ἀδελφὸς) and Col 4:7 (ἀγαπητὸς ἀδελφὸς). In Col 4:9 Onesimus is referred to as ἀγαπητῷ ἀδελφῷ, paralleling Philemon.[34] In both cases, the phrase likely depends on a similar one in 1 Cor 15:58. There are other thematic parallels here with Colossians as well (Col 3:22 ordering slaves to obey according to the flesh, σάρκα, the flesh also tying Onesimus and Philemon, see Phlm 16 σαρκὶ).[35]

Philemon 23–24 is notably similar to Col 4:10–15. The names of Mark, Aristarchus, Luke, and Demas all occur in similar succession.[36] Aristarchus and Epaphrus are both referred to as συναιχμάλωτός ("fellow prisoner"), while the others are συνεργοί ("coworkers" or "fellow workers"). Notably, the phraseology is somewhat closer to "fellow prisoner" (with three words in succession shared: ὁ συναιχμάλωτός μου).

Phlm 25 can be found verbatim in Phil 4:23 (Ἡ χάρις τοῦ κυρίου Ἰησοῦ Χριστοῦ μετὰ τοῦ πνεύματος ὑμῶν). Only Phil 4:23 and Phlm 25 have this word-for-word agreement indicating a potential literary connection, though it is close enough to other Pauline outro salutations that we might consider it copied from Paul's usual style.[37] As noted above, the notion that Paul was sitting in prison and copying from his previous letters strains credulity. Verhoef's work establishing the principal core authentic epistles determined that Philippians belongs to the "authentic" corpus of Pauline letters.[38] As such, Philemon appears to be the outlier for our purposes.

Other issues pervade Colossians and Philemon. Col 1:1–4 renders "you" in the plural (ὑμῶν), but Phlm 4 alters this to the singular to fit the personal letter style (σου). This shift, I believe, indicates an editorial process. The change from plural "you" in Phlm 3 (ὑμῖν) to a singular "you" in Phlm 4 without denoting a change of referent is rather jarring and unexplained, unless we posit that this passage was edited imperfectly to fit the single

34. Van den Bergh van Eysinga, "Paulus' Brief aan Philemon," 13. In the authentic epistles, he speaks of "my beloved brethren," such as Phil 4:1 (ἀδελφοί μου ἀγαπητοὶ) and 1 Cor 15:58 (ἀδελφοί μου ἀγαπητοί).

35. Cf. Eph 6:9. See Van den Bergh van Eysinga, "Paulus' Brief aan Philemon," 13.

36. Paley, "Questioning the Pauline Authorship of Philemon," 16–17; Van Manen, *Wave of Hypercriticism*, 148; Steck, "Plinius im Neuen Testament," 572; Van den Bergh van Eysinga, "Paulus' Brief aan Philemon," 13; McKnight, *Letter to Philemon*, 111–13; A. Thompson, *Colossians and Philemon*, 254–55; Patzia, *Ephesians, Colossians, Philemon*, 99–102; Seesengood, *Philemon*, 19–26; Pao, *Colossians & Philemon*, 421–23.

37. Gal 6:18 has Ἡ χάρις τοῦ κυρίου ἡμῶν Ἰησοῦ Χριστοῦ μετὰ τοῦ πνεύματος ὑμῶν, ἀδελφοί· ἀμήν, which is the next closest parallel. Cf. 2 Cor 13:13. See Van den Bergh van Eysinga, "Paulus' Brief aan Philemon," 13.

38. Verhoef, "Determining the Authenticity of the Paulines."

subject style of a personal letter while the rest emulates Paul's general style of referring to a congregation (Phlm 2–3).[39] This intermixing of singular and plural, notably, was problematic enough that later scribes altered it to harmonize the text.[40]

One other argument (discussed in chapter 2) is that the narrative of Colossians would not make sense were it based on Philemon, whereas Philemon makes *more* sense if based on Colossians. This is because Colossians presupposes Paul's lack of familiarity with people at Colossae, while Philemon has an assumed established house church in the background. Philemon being so small, it would be impossible to miss that he had friends in Colossae. However, if Philemon is based on Colossians, a much larger text, it would be more sensible that the author missed or forgot Col 2:1. Likewise, Epaphras is not mentioned as a prisoner in Colossians but is in Philemon. If Philemon were written prior to Colossians, we again have to explain why the author of Colossians missed this, whereas if Philemon is cribbing from Colossians but taking place *after*, then Epaphras' imprisonment is assumed in the interim. As such, on multiple grounds Philemon makes more sense as being based on Colossians than vice versa.

As Luke Timothy Johnson discusses in *Constructing Paul*, the teachings in Colossians and Philemon seem to reinforce each other, specifically on the treatment of and Christian disposition toward slaves.[41] This close relationship again suggests that they must have some kind of intertextual relationship, in addition to the many linguistic elements noted above. Taken in context, we can argue that Philemon seems to have expanded upon Colossians' teachings about master-slave relations in 3:22—4:1. In both, the primary instruction for master-slave relations is to put them in the context of their relationship to God, i.e., to not create division as they are brothers in Christ. This is not to dismantle the social statuses of slaves and their owners, but to remove divisions within the cultic community. Were Colossians based on Philemon, a text that gives these detailed instructions, it is peculiar that Paul would address Onesimus without ever mentioning his

39. Van Manen, *Wave of Hypercriticism*, 147–48. Van Manen's suggestion that the shift of speaker number indicates internal problems is less convincing, as "I" and "we" interchange quite freely in ancient letters.

40. For instance, per Nestle-Aland Twenty-Eighth edition, verse 6 instead of ἐν ἡμῖν (textus receptus) others (e.g., F and G) read εν υμιν. In verse 7, instead of πολλὴν ἔσχον other manuscripts have πολλην εσχομεν.

41. Johnson, *Constructing Paul*, 262–66. See also MacDonald, "Kinship and Family in the New Testament World," 38–40.

owner, whom Paul would have also known by name. Philemon's absence is better understood if Onesimus is transformed into a slave after the fact.[42]

Lastly, it is tough to see why Colossians would copy from Philemon at all. The letter to Philemon was rather obscure, with no author even quoting it until the third century. Proposing Colossians is a forgery based on Philemon, as was done in the past, is a tough ask. If even the church fathers quoting from Paul's letters do not seem to know or quote Philemon (even when it would suit them on digressions about slaves[43]), why would one think that Colossians would quote this obscure letter? If, however, we propose that Colossians-Philemon circulated together, the best explanation (regardless of whether we think Paul wrote these letters) is that Philemon is probably reliant upon Colossians. Given the contradictions between the two, it is also difficult to imagine them being codependent (i.e., written at the same time).

This is not the sum total of relations that point to Philemon being reliant on other letters (Schwab's volume in particular should be consulted for more depth).[44] However, I believe the above evidence is enough to conclude, at minimum, that Philemon and Colossians share a close literary relationship, and that Philemon also has a relationship to 1 Corinthians. That a prisoner, whose life could be imperiled at any minute, was drafting new letters that copied older ones he had sent to previous congregations seems unlikely (as noted in chapter 2). In view of this, I propose that the following model of dependency best explains the origins of the letters to Philemon, Colossians, and Ephesians: 1 Corinthians was used to partly compose Colossians; Philemon was composed using Colossians and 1 Corinthians, possibly by the same person who composed Colossians; and Ephesians was composed primarily relying on Colossians.

---

42. The counter proposition, that Colossians presupposes Onesimus has been freed/manumitted is unlikely, since the letter to Philemon implies that Onesimus would return and be of high utility to Philemon as a slave again (Phlm 11). Additionally, there may have been no avenue to free such a slave, see Green, "Paul's Letter to Philemon."

43. E.g., Ignatius, *Letter to Polycarp* 4.3, 6.2; *Didache* 4.9–11; and *1 Clement* 61.1–4.

44. Schwab, *Echtheitskritische Untersuchungen zu den vier kleineren Paulusbriefen*, 88–199.

REMARKS ON LANGUAGE

The language of Philemon could, on the surface, indicate that it was written by a separate author. However, it must be admitted that a *majority* of the "oddities" I have pointed to above are mere grammatical variations of words that appear throughout the Pauline and non-Pauline corpuses. As a result, the majority is rather indeterminate. However, there are more striking elements that potentially speak to inauthenticity. We have seen some evidence of this with the verbatim overlaps with Colossians and apparent reliance on 1 Corinthians. It appears that 1 Corinthians may have been particularly influential, given their many shared terms (as seen above). While it seems rather suspect and incredible to think of Paul as copying letters he had already sent off from within a prison cell (see chapter 2),[45] the same cannot be said of another author with Paul's already extant corpus sat comfortably in front of him.

This explains Philemon's various parallels in language with the authentic Paulines, but especially the closeness it exhibits with Colossians. If the trio are regarded as being from the same author, which seems evident by the copying of language exhibited between them (not to mention shared characters, setting, and themes), we can deduce that this single writer predominantly worked from 1 Corinthians, Galatians, and Philippians. This would provide the setting of the imprisonment, account for the shared language, and further explain the exhibited discrepancies.

The preponderance of terms shared makes a possible relationship with 1 Corinthians particularly likely (see above). What I find especially striking, though, is that several terms that appear in Philemon also appear in chapter 7 of 1 Corinthians, close to where 1 Corinthians discusses slavery. The relationship between Philemon and Colossians is likewise quite strong, with numerous terms and forms only shared between them and passages that appear to be verbatim. That Philemon is from the same author as

---

45. As discussed previously, and to reiterate, "During their confinement, prisoners could be tortured and maltreated in different ways, both by guards and by their fellow prisoners. Torture, including forms of food deprivation, isolation and continuous enchainment was often used as a way to gain evidence and confessions, and to discover the involvement of other people in the criminal act. It was thus a common experience for those who were accused of a crime" (see Neutel and Smit, "Paul, Imprisonment and Crisis," 31). The idea that Paul (or some follower) carefully snuck in his pervious letters and copied from them under these horrific conditions paints an absurd picture. It is simply unprecedented among the authentic prison epistles I am aware of in Greco-Roman literature.

Colossians and that they both pull from Galatians seems likely, especially considering that Col 3:11 looks almost identical (with some modification) to Gal 3:28. It appears that both Philemon and Colossians looked at Paul's authentic epistles and copied what suited them. This level of copying is, to my knowledge, unheard of among known authentic epistles from other authors, much less those written from prison.

As Bart Ehrman remarks, this similar type of copying is a telltale sign of inauthenticity, such as 2 Thessalonians mimicking the style and layout of 1 Thessalonians.[46] As Ehrman relays, "The easiest places to imitate the style and wording of a letter are its beginning and ending . . ."[47] We see this in Philemon's salutations, where we have numerous places of verbatim agreements between Philemon and other letters in the Pauline corpus (as noted above). We also see this in other pseudo-Pauline (and related) forgeries.[48] Using the same standards that Bart Ehrman applies to 2 Thessalonians,[49] we have some (albeit weak) linguistic reasons for considering Philemon to

46. Ehrman, *Forgery and Counterforgery*, 159–60. Campbell, *Framing Paul*, 204–16 lobbies for 2 Thessalonians' authenticity, though I do not find the arguments particularly convincing. In the most recent analysis by Savoy ("Authorship of Pauline Epistles Revisited"), 1 and 2 Thessalonians form a group separate from the *Hauptbriefe* stylistically (with Colossians-Ephesians being another group, possibly from the same author, and the Pastorals also being in their own group). While the Corinthian letters seem to have a relationship with 1 Thessalonians, according to Savoy ("Authorship Study on the Letters of Saint Paul"), 2 Thessalonians is a greater outlier; a recent thesis by Katarina Laken indicates that vocabulary richness factors (which are difficult to replicate in forgery) notably differentiate 2 Thessalonians from 1 Thessalonians. As such, stylometric analysis hardly rules singularly in favor of 2 Thessalonians. Further, Kreinecker, "Imitation Hypothesis," has demonstrated using documentary papyri and verbal forms among both them and the Pauline epistles that 2 Thessalonians deviates significantly in ways we would not expect from Paul but would from an imitated, exaggerated Pauline style. So, even without stylometry, there appear to be other methods of detecting failure points in 2 Thessalonians' concealed inauthenticity. Likewise, one can point to several entries in Brodie et al., eds., *Intertextuality of the Epistles*, 133–207.

47. Ehrman, *Forgery and Counterforgery*, 158. This also greatly effects Schenk, "Brief des Paulus an Philemon in der neureren Forschung," 3442–45, cited by Dunn, *Epistles to the Colossians and to Philemon*, 299–300; and Bartchy, "Philemon," 306. Schenk's argumentation relies in no small part on the introductions being supposedly Pauline, when these are in fact the easiest portions to forge, alongside the very typical and ubiquitous Pauline phrases that other forgeries contain.

48. Soon, "Before Deception," 435–36 discusses Salvian's *Ad ecclesiam*, which mimics Paul's self-descriptions and salutations. Third Corinthians likewise does this, as does the apocryphal *Epistle to the Laodiceans*, whose prescript is likely cribbed from Galatians 1; see Tite, "Dusting Off a Pseudo-Historical Letter," 292.

49. Ehrman, *Forgery and Counterforgery*, 158–71.

be an inauthentic letter. In my view, the author is either the same as that of Colossians or is aware of their work, along with the other authentic Pauline epistles. Colossians itself likely has some relationship to 1 Corinthians as well, indicating Philemon and Colossians could have been composed together by someone who knew 1 Corinthians. This might be Paul, but it might be a forger. To be certain, the authenticity of either Colossians or Philemon would need to be answered definitively. The two letters' authenticities are comingled. If Philemon is authentic, we have good cause to think that Colossians is as well. If Philemon is inauthentic, so too might Colossians be. As Gordon Fee once remarked, "It remains one of the singular mysteries of NT scholarship that so many scholars reject Pauline authorship of Colossians yet affirm the authenticity of Philemon."[50] As noted in chapter 2, we have several reasons to consider Philemon as having been written *after* Colossians, particularly internal narrative reasons. As the two letters overlap so significantly, we ought to conclude that these narrative elements are, in fact, important.

This all has direct ramifications regarding potential reasons for why this letter was forged. Philemon gains its prison imagery from the existing tradition of Paul's imprisonment—a type scene for forged letters—but uses far more oblique language than "authentic" Paul generally does. Unlike the Paul of Philippians, Philemon's "Paul" sees no need to disguise his status as a prisoner; this Paul uses blanket terms and other elements that seem to betray an utter lack of urgency.

All of this said, I do not think the stylistic issues previously remarked upon are completely determinative. Authors can, in fact, diverge from their own styles depending on genre and other conditions (such as aging and emotionality). As a result, we should expect some variation. Basing a case on stylistic considerations is a dangerous pursuit, as recent studies have demonstrated. Additionally, we could easily point out the *similarities* (whereas here I have focused primarily on *dissimilarities*) between Philemon and other Pauline letters.[51] Ultimately, style is mostly indeterminate due to such a small sample size, and each individual reader must choose how to weigh the evidence presented.

Perhaps the strongest evidence against Pauline authorship is that Philemon shares so many overlaps with Colossians, which arguably make the most sense if one imagines either them having been written together or

50. Fee, *Pauline Christology*, 289n2.
51. Brookins, *Ancient Rhetoric and the Style of Paul's Letters*.

Philemon being based on Colossians.[52] Even in antiquity, overlaps between Philemon and Colossians were recognized,[53] so their authenticity rises and falls together; if Colossians cannot be conclusively demonstrated as Pauline on matters of style, then neither can Philemon. Considering that, up to this point, the authenticity of Colossians has largely relied on the presumed authenticity of Philemon, we have a situation where, arguably, neither can be established as authentically Pauline on style alone.

RETURNING TO VERHOEF'S MODEL

It is important now to return to the framework I operate under in this volume. Verhoef's model for authenticity explicitly requires that the contents of a letter cohere in terms of vocabulary and style with those of authentic Pauline letters. However, the language of Philemon is not as consistent within the authentic Pauline corpus as was previously declared. Philemon contains a number of *hapax legomena* relative to its exceptionally small size, in addition to seemingly unique phrases, while also displaying (in my view) clear evidence of having been copied from previous letters. Therefore, much of its similar verbal correspondences can be explained by Philemon being a forgery that directly copies authentic Pauline work.

As seen above, the largest overlaps between Philemon and the authentic Paulines occur in the openings and closings, the two places that are (as Ehrman relates) easiest to imitate the style of an author. Meanwhile, the middle of the letter is highly variant but consistently displays a relationship with Colossians (especially with rarer word forms), plus a lighter one with 1 Corinthians' section on slavery. At various points it even resembles the Pastorals.

Philemon is so variant and has so many affinities with generally dismissed Paulines that we are left to conclude that, based on the evidence we have, it cannot be validated as an authentic letter with linguistics alone. However, given the verbatim overlaps that indicate copying from Colossians and 1 Corinthians, the conclusion of inauthenticity seems far more

52. This is the position of several academics who take Colossians and Philemon as authentic; see Beale, *Colossians and Philemon*, 8; Pao, *Colossians & Philemon*, 23, etc.

53. Theodoret of Cyrus, *Commentary on Philemon* translated in Hill, *Theodoret of Cyrus*, 261–65; John Chrysostom, *Homilies on Philemon*. For modern scholars, see A. Thompson, *Colossians and Philemon*, 5; Hamm, *Philippians, Colossians, Philemon*, 154; Patzia, *Ephesians, Colossians, Philemon*, 10; Pao, *Colossians & Philemon*, 22–23; Fitzmyer, *Letter to Philemon*, 9; Beale, *Colossians and Philemon*, 8.

likely than not. At the very least, we are obliged to be agnostic about its authenticity based on language and style. In the next chapter, I will discuss potential reasons for why this letter may have been forged.

While many contend that the letter is too small for any usable stylometric analysis (below), during more than one analysis it was found to have fallen outside the generally accepted style of Pauline letters.[54] Notably, this is also true of Colossians and Ephesians, according to Savoy's study. Further, claims that these findings are invalid are more and more hampered by a growing number of studies that account for authenticity and authorship using smaller and smaller sample sizes.[55] It can be grouped on its own or with other non-Pauline letters depending on methodology, but again the evidence from a hand comparison, like mine, and stylometric analyses line up. Philemon's language and style cannot be considered typically Pauline at first blush. On the other hand, various sociohistorical considerations could nullify most of these issues; age, situation, context, and genre all play roles in literature production and, as a result, could all affect the outcomes

54. Savoy, "Authorship of Pauline Epistles Revisited." Mark Bilby and K. Lance Lotharp privately shared findings from a principal components analysis of morphological tags, finding a cluster with canonical Philemon, 1 Timothy, and Titus. This finding, again, puts Philemon on the outer limits of what is generally considered Pauline in discussing authentic literature. In another recent study, Van der Ventel and Newman applied term frequency–inverse document frequency to the Pauline corpus, with Philemon and Titus forming the lower bound of the similarity index ("Application of the Term Frequency-Inverse Document Frequency," 264). In a recent study, Kroonenberg (*Multivariate Humanities*, 156) calls for a closer relationship between Philemon and 1 Thessalonians, but that the authenticity of these two (i.e., if they were written by Paul) is more difficult to ascertain based on the data.

55. Campbell, *Framing Paul*, 259 contends that sample sizes of around five hundred at minimum are needed, but more recent studies, as pointed out by Tuccinardi, perform accurate tests of authenticity utilizing word sizes limited to Twitter "tweets" (which have a 280-character limit); see Tuccinardi, "Application," which applies such methods to the Plinian correspondences with Trajan. Tuccinardi comes away with the conclusion that Pliny's *Ep.* 10.96–97 are inauthentic due to variances detected with an *n*-gram model, though I find this to be problematic. *N*-gram models are based on predicting what would most likely be written based on previous work, but because 10.96–97 cover new content and contexts this would be outside the predictive parameters to begin with—of course the model has reason to consider them inauthentic. This is part of the issue with many stylometric analyses. Campbell is not alone either; see Neumann, *Authenticity*, 124; Mealand, "Extent of the Pauline Corpus," 65.

described here, as Van Nes argues with the Pastoral Epistles.[56] However, as Savoy's research shows, Van Nes is hardly the final word on the subject.[57]

Further, the epistle to Philemon is of such a small sample size that we cannot currently make many secure judgments about its inauthenticity on the basis of style and grammar.[58] If this is the case, though, we must also do away with all claims and statements about Philemon being Pauline in character.[59] Still, in a recent analysis applying cosine similarity to Paul's letters, Philemon came up rather variant. Roy and Robertson thus propose:

> . . . while we may defensibly conclude that Paul—along with a scribe—could have simply written this letter in a manner atypical relative to the other surviving letters, our quantitative findings might suggest other explanations: that this letter was mostly composed by a scribe, or perhaps that it was composed by someone else in Paul's circle.[60]

As such, stylometry is certainly not settled where Philemon is concerned. The knife cuts both ways on issues of sample size; if a sample size is too small to indicate inauthenticity, it is likewise too small to indicate authenticity. Thus, any claims that this letter is an exemplar of "Paul's" style and vocabulary are as unconvincing as claims to the contrary. Regarding grammar and vocabulary, we should remain agnostic and instead look to other issues pertaining to the letter's authenticity, such as its themes and literary

---

56. Van Nes, *Pauline Language and the Pastoral Epistles*. Of course, Van Nes' conclusion that some epistles (including Philemon) bear more hallmarks of literary productions than of oral dictations also gives some room for pause, since oral dictation is precisely what we would expect in an imprisonment scenario.

57. One can find a few issues with Van Nes' study (*Pauline Language and the Pastoral Epistles*). For instance, while textuality/orality might theoretically explain some differences in the Pastorals' style from other letters, we may also note that dictation and orality was common in composition, particularly where slaves were used (Moss, "Secretary"). If a forger used a slave (quite plausible) as a secretary, this would account for variation. Thus, textuality/orality could not adequately explain differences between the Pastorals and other Pauline epistles. This is one of many caveats I have for Van Nes' study.

58. This reservation is noted by Savoy (cited above) and Neumann, *Authenticity*, 124. Meanwhile, a few others have attempted to conclude it authentic using statistical analysis, such as Kenny, *Stylometric Study of the New Testament*, who ultimately concludes twelve of the thirteen letters ascribed to Paul are authentic (excluding Titus).

59. Stuhlmacher, *Brief an Philemon*, 19–20; Fitzmyer, *Letter to Philemon*, 8; Dunn, *Epistles to the Colossians and to Philemon*, 299–300; A. Thompson, *Colossians and Philemon*, 5; Patzia, *Ephesians, Colossians, Philemon*, 10, etc.

60. Roy and Robertson, "Applying Cosine Similarity," 111.

content. The evidence of intertextuality with the other Pauline epistles, though, certainly begins to stack against Philemon's authenticity, in my view.

We must conclude either that (A) language and style are enough to make judgments on authorship, in which case we must also admit that this letter has many strange features for something so tiny and further that stylometric and hand analyses have not deemed it typically Pauline, or that (B) its language and style are not enough on which to judge authorship on, in which case it cannot be utilized as a basis for the authenticity of other epistles like Colossians.[61] Either way, we cannot conclude that this letter is Pauline in style or language, nor can we necessarily conclude it is un-Pauline either. As authenticity is not a valid default assumption (see chapter 1), on stylistic grounds we must remain agnostic. However, the evidence of intertextual relations between Colossians and Philemon (with Philemon, in my view, being reliant on the former) points more toward inauthenticity.

61. This would have significant ramifications, since much of the defense of Colossians' authenticity hinges on Philemon being authentic.

4

A Second Century Proposal

FORGERIES DO NOT APPEAR in a vacuum—they develop out of specific situations and contexts that create opportunity or necessity for their existence. This means that if I posit Philemon is a forgery, I should be able to give some reason as to how and why that occurred.

Scholars, both past and present, have had difficulty imagining any scenario under which Philemon could have been forged, which in turn helps form the consensus of authenticity; the letter is so innocuous that many find it impossible to consider forgery, and if one cannot demonstrate motivations for forgery, then there is no reason to presume forgery occurred. I dub this argument for authenticity the "objection from innocuousness." This focuses on the binary thinking (authentic vs. inauthentic) that I have critiqued above and ignores that something could plausibly be a forgery without us knowing why it was forged. When working with limited data, we should make room for such notions.

This is hardly a compelling justification for my position. That we have an excuse for why no apparent reason exists does not itself prove there was a reason. As such, this chapter aims to discuss the following: (1) slavery in early Christianity and the development of debates on regulating slaves, (2) evidence for dating the epistle and its relation to slave debates in early Christianity, (3) potential motivations for why the letter would be forged in light of the above, and then (4) a reassessment of the objection from innocuousness.

SLAVERY, EARLY CHRISTIANITY, AND PHILEMON

There is little doubt in my mind that this letter had nothing to do with manumission. Green's recent analysis of ancient Roman law indicates that the manumission of a runaway slave (or a slave who had incurred some kind of damages to their owner) would not have made sense.[1] To the contrary, manumission would have all but condemned someone to an even lower status than that of an enslaved person.[2] With this in mind, the concept of manumission is likely out of the question when understanding Philemon, authentic or not.[3] Instead, the letter seems to negotiate slave-master relations.

Ancient Christians interpreted this letter rather uniformly: "Paul" advocated that a slave be returned to his master, not for a sweeping change to the class hierarchy. Furthermore, it implies that the slave would be of greater utility now that he was converted. On this matter, John Chrysostom's comments are particularly enlightening:

> Secondly, that we ought not to abandon the race of slaves, even if they have proceeded to extreme wickedness. For if a thief and a runaway become so virtuous that Paul was willing to make him a companion, and says in this Epistle, "that in thy stead he might have ministered unto me" (v. 13), much more ought we not abandon the free. Thirdly, that we ought not to withdraw slaves from the service to their masters. For if Paul, who had such confidence in Philemon, was unwilling to detain Onesimus, so useful and serviceable to minister to himself, without the consent of his master, much less ought we so to act. For if the servant is so excellent, he ought by all means to continue in that service, and to acknowledge the authority of his master, that he may be the occasion of

---

1. Green, "Paul's Letter to Philemon."

2. As Green states, "So, some kind of manumission was possible for Onesimus, but into what status we do not know. If he was under thirty, as is likely, that probably rules out formal manumission at the time of the letter. If he had ever been severely punished, that rules out joining the *Latini Juniani* too, but left open the remaining option to the status of the *dediticii*" ("Paul's Letter to Philemon," 98, emphasis original).

3. To be sure, nothing in any of Paul's letters suggests that Paul believed in demolishing the institution of slavery. While 1 Cor 7 has oft been considered evidence of a call for reform, recent analysis indicates that no social class changes are necessarily implied by his wording; see Økland, "Textual Reproduction as Surplus Value," 191; Boer and Petterson, "Hand of the Master," 146–48. For another curious case of how Paul potentially handled slavery, see Marchal, "Slaves as Wo/men and Unmen."

benefit to all in that house. Why dost thou take the candle from the candlestick to place it in a bushel?[4]

Other ancient Christian commentaries are no different in their affirmation that this epistle supports Christians owning not just slaves, but other Christians; at the very least, they see no need to challenge the ownership of slaves by Christians.[5] Chrysostom's notion of a "race of slaves" parallels authors like Aristotle, who regarded slaves as naturally and inherently bound to their role, born to be such.[6] Meanwhile, Theodore of Mopsuestia concludes that the letter demands no change in people's status. In fact, Theodore is adamant that Paul wished for people to know their place in society and maintain the status quo (continue acquiescing to Caesar and his law and such), so long as they maintain the spark of "true religion" within them that marks their Christianity.[7]

As Paul's other generally accepted six letters seem to indicate, discussions and issues regarding slavery were not much of an issue in the early church, at least not one he saw fit to address in detail. This could be due to a lower economic status among nascent Christian communities, which meant a lower likelihood of owning slaves at all.[8] During the Principate, aside from the urban areas of Rome and Athens, it is estimated that slave prices were rather high in relation to wages.[9] Scheidel remarks:

> I suspect that slave markets may have been limited in scope: Greek states that relied on more archaic forms of bondage had lower incentives to bid for slaves; and even within the "slave-society" poleis of central Greece, only a limited proportion of the population would control sufficient resources to invest in chattel slaves.[10]

4. John Chrysostom, *Homilies on Philemon*, argumentum. Translation from Schaff, ed., *Select Library*, 546.

5. Ambrosiaster's *Commentary on Philemon*, translated in Bray, *Commentaries on Galatians–Philemon*, 161–63.

6. For discussion, see Fortenbaugh, *Aristotle's Practical Side*, 241–47.

7. Theodore of Mopsuestia, *Commentary on Philemon*, translated in Greer, *Commentary on the Minor Pauline Epistles*, 772–85.

8. This is not to say early Christ followers did not possess slaves (some certainly did), but that there were probably so few that they would have been of no concern to Paul. However, it is notable that when Pliny the Younger (*Ep.* 96) sought out Christians, he primarily targeted slaves. It is not clear from his own account how far Christian beliefs had spread amongst the slave-holding class.

9. Scheidel, "Real Slave Prices."

10. Scheidel, "Real Slave Prices," 15.

In Roman Egypt, slaves were rarer. Most households could not afford slaves, and those that did had one or two at most.[11] The price of an unskilled slave would have been equivalent to two and a half years worth of wages for the average rural worker, according to Scheidel.[12] Given the indications that nascent Christianity predominantly spread among the lower classes, it is fair to conclude that most early Christians did not own slaves.[13]

Aside from his comments in 1 Cor 7, the evidence that Paul would have cared much about slaves as a class of individuals, much less their general treatment, is lacking. As such, the issue of master-slave relations probably belongs best in a post-Pauline environment, when early Christianity had achieved a larger following amongst the slave-owning classes, thus necessitating a prolonged discussion on the subject.[14] Glancy discusses the rising discussion of slaves among Christians during the second century, which would have been a prime time to mention Paul's letter to Philemon had it existed and/or circulated.[15] Yet those like Justin Martyr, who complained of fabrications against Christians (i.e., that non-Christians were torturing the slaves of Christians and then laying blame on the owners; see *First Apology* 2.12.4), never quote nor reference Paul's little epistle, which surely would have provided exonerating evidence (especially "Paul's" message of Philemon returning as a "brother").

Issues concerning the relationship between Christians and slavery were much more at home in the second century CE. While 1 Cor 7 never elaborates on the treatment of slaves, the disputed epistles do (Col 3:22—4:1; Eph 6:5–9; 1 Tim 6:1–2). Of those, 1 Timothy likely dates to the second century, being (along with the other Pastorals) anti-Marcionite content.[16] At this same time, Ignatius' *Letter to Polycarp* 4.3, 6.2; *Didache*

---

11. Scheidel, "Real Slave Prices," 14

12. Scheidel, "Real Slave Prices, 8.

13. This is not to say that slavery was not widespread. Boer and Petterson, *Time of Troubles*, 113 estimate that at least 10 percent of the entire population of the Roman Empire were slaves, and the percentages would vary even more drastically depending on environment (i.e., the urban polis, where slaves and slave markets were plentiful, versus the rural, where affording a slave was much more difficult).

14. For instance, as Glancy, *Slavery in Early Christianity*, 130 notes, the first (reliable) record of early Christians in Pliny, *Ep.* 10.96 indicates that he tortured Christian slaves while governing Bithynia-Pontus. This city had a rather dominant Christian population, enough to cause economic problems that concerned Pliny.

15. Glancy, *Slavery in Early Christianity*, 131.

16. Campbell, *Framing Paul*, 368–85.

4.9–11; and *1 Clement* 61.1–4 also give some instruction, as do a few other second-century texts.[17] Thus, a text providing rather detailed instructions on handling a rift between master and slave would find greater utility in the second century. All of this provides some background that may influence how we determine the *terminus a quo* and *terminus ad quem* for Philemon.

Furthermore, we should note that Philemon's portrayal of slave and master relations does not seem to reflect historical situations (as discussed in chapter 2). Philemon seems to have converted at Paul's behest prior to the Letter to Philemon being written (v. 19), but as was discussed prior, a family patriarch's conversion to a new faith or allegiance typically meant that the rest of the household (including slaves) followed suit. Onesimus having been converted separately while Paul was in chains (v. 10) would be exceptional, meaning that we are perhaps dealing with ahistorical fiction. Thus, again, the letter can be disentangled from its traditionally presumed first-century setting in Colossae.

DATE RANGES FOR PHILEMON

A *Terminus a Quo*

Early evidence for placing Philemon in the first century is rather scarce, but it is also problematic to place the letter in just about any specific time frame. As noted in chapters 2 and 3, the text has rather significant literary parallels with other Pauline epistles, but the closest is Colossians, for which it shares numerous names and verbatim overlaps with various passages. The other text with which Philemon shares relations is 1 Corinthians. There are many ways to explain these overlaps: (1) Philemon is reliant upon Colossians and/or 1 Corinthians; (2) Colossians and/or 1 Corinthians are reliant on Philemon; (3) Philemon and Colossians were written jointly and reliant on 1 Corinthians; (4) 1 Corinthians is jointly reliant on Colossians and Philemon.

These are all possible, which poses a problem when trying to decide between them. This also depends on whether we regard the literary overlaps between 1 Corinthians as significant enough to warrant concluding that Philemon relies upon them. While not firm, I would suggest that if 1 Corinthians were reliant upon Philemon/Colossians, we would see more verbal agreement in the places of parallel noted above (chapter 3). For

17. Fitzmyer, *Letter to Philemon*, 33.

instance, in sections with verbatim agreements, Paul tends to be consistent (i.e., certain greetings). Therefore, Philemon's shift from addressing a letter to a single house unit or man (Philemon) into the plural congregation (where the verbatim overlaps occur) may be evidence that the letter pulls from where the plural usage is more common, i.e., past letters like Colossians or 1 Corinthians. Given Philemon's agreements with 1 Corinthians in other places, alongside Colossians', my suggestion is that 1 Corinthians was utilized by whoever drafted Philemon-Colossians. This means that, on the assumption of authenticity, we can assign a *terminus a quo* of around 50 CE as Campbell argued in *Framing Paul*,[18] though one could certainly take issue with his methodology and conclusions.[19]

A few literary elements may tip this scale, the first being the theme of imprisonment. Given the internally inconsistent portrayal of Paul's imprisonment, it seems unlikely to me that this letter was truly written from prison. If not, then why use that setting? One answer can be found in the fact that the prison setting (and the fascination with Paul's imprisonments) was a specific feature of late-first- and second-century Christian literature. 2 Tim 1:8[20] makes use of this setting, as do Col 4:3; Eph 3:1; and 3 Cor 1.[21] There are also the seven imprisonments mentioned in 1 Clement 5.5–6 and the one mentioned in Polycarp's *Letter to the Philippians* 9. The second century is also when the myths of persecution began taking shape, which codified an interest in both that setting and understanding their first apostles' sufferings.[22]

As discussed above, slavery became a specific issue in the second century. At that time, several church leaders and texts were concerned with instructing on the treatment and handling of slaves (as well as master-slave relations). One would think that if a Pauline letter dealing with this topic were floating around, these authors would have used it to their advantage (and were it circulating with Colossians from the first century CE, there is

---

18. Campbell, *Framing Paul*, 258.

19. Bernier, "When Paul Met Sergius."

20. Campbell, *Framing Paul*, 368–85 makes a good argument for a second[century anti-Marcionite context for the text. Some have even suggested that Polycarp of Smyrna authored the text, see Von Campenhausen, *Aus der Frühzeit des Christentums*, 197–252.

21. Even later, we can note the problematic *Epistle to the Laodiceans*.

22. I have published extensively on this topic; see Hansen, "Problem of Annals 15.44" and "Number of the Myth." See also, Moss, *Myth of Persecution*; Shaw, "Myth of the Neronian Persecution."

a good chance they might have it). Given this, its absence from their work is suspicious and potentially points to an even later origin for Philemon.

We might add one other element: the mention of the apostle Luke (v. 23). It has been largely overlooked that outside of these currently challenged texts (Philemon, Colossians, and 2 Timothy), the apostle Luke is never mentioned as a companion to Paul. In fact, there is no convincing evidence that Christians even knew of Luke's existence until after Justin Martyr was writing.[23] The figure of Luke may have evolved into a Pauline coworker in the second century and was only later adopted as author of the eponymous gospel. This would account for Luke not being mentioned as the supposed author of the gospel early on,[24] and it would further cohere with the late attestation of all these epistles. In short, it could well be argued based on this evidence that Luke's presence provides grounds for dating the letter into the second century.[25]

A final note is Outi Leppä's argument that Colossians may have some knowledge or reliance on the Gospel of Mark.[26] Though tentative, this would ensure a hard date after 70 CE for the composition of Colossians, and the composition of Philemon by extension.

The mere setting of the Epistle to Philemon is, arguably, reason to suspect a second-century dating for its composition. However, no firm *terminus a quo* can be assigned due to the speculative nature of this evidence. If authentic, the Letter to Philemon likely dates prior to roughly 65 CE, when Paul is typically dated as dying.[27] If inauthentic, it could date within the same time frame or as late as the second century. However, though speculative, I would consider the accumulation of all the above to point to a late-first or early-second-century dating as the best *terminus a quo* for Philemon.

23. Luke is not mentioned by Ignatius, Polycarp, 1 or 2 Clement, the *Epistle of Barnabas*, the fragments of Papias, Quadratus, *Epistle to Diognetus*, *Shepherd of Hermas*, the *Didache*, or the *Martyrdom of Polycarp*. Luke is never mentioned by Justin Martyr's surviving works, or in the *Acts of Paul and Thecla*. As such, it seems that the tradition of Paul having an accompanying partner named Luke is unattested in early Christian non-canonical literature in the second half of the second century.

24. Kok, "Justin Martyr and the Authorship of Luke's Gospel."

25. This works even more so with comparison to the Pastorals, which contain an anti-Marcionite edge; see Campbell, *Framing Paul*, 392–403.

26. Leppä, *Making of Colossians*, 256–59.

27. Assuming we consider such dating valid or reasonable.

A *Terminus ad Quem*

The unfortunate reality is that our historical record holds scarce evidence of Philemon. The first person to explicitly mention it was Tertullian, who claimed it was in Marcion's *Apostolikon* and unaltered.[28] Because we know not what Tertullian's copy of Philemon looked like, we know not what "unaltered" means; unaltered to Tertullian does not mean unaltered for the *textus receptus*.

Campbell suggests utilizing the Marcionite collection as evidence for the earliest shape of the Pauline corpus.[29] I disagree, especially as we have no attestation of the *Apostolikon*'s full contents prior to Tertullian. All we know is that by the time of Tertullian, it had this shape and contents; we cannot rule out that the influence of other Christianities manipulated (A) how the texts were ordered and (B) which texts were (or became) included. As such, we can only securely date Philemon's existence to, at the earliest, the late second century. In this case, we only know that the Marcionite text Tertullian used in his own time had acquired Philemon, but extrapolating behind that is questionable, especially given Philemon's reception in other early compilations of Paul's letters (see introduction).

There is, however, one other text that is often said to parallel Philemon. Ignatius's *Letter to the Ephesians* (traditionally dated to the early second century, though some doubts exist[30]) specifically refers to a figure named Onesimus. Knox contends that there are enough similarities between the letters to warrant concluding that Ignatius is indebted to Philemon.[31] If correct, and assuming the Ignatian corpus's authenticity, this could warrant one thinking Philemon is authentically Pauline, given the early attestation. However, I see several issues with this and consider the "parallels" to be strenuous. The only overlap I agree has any force is that Ignatius and "Paul" both make similar puns out of Onesimus' name. Most

---

28. Tertullian, *Against Marcion* 5.21.

29. Campbell, *Framing Paul*, 387–92.

30. Lookadoo, "Date and Authenticity of the Ignatian Letters"; Detering, *Fabricated Paul*, 86–98; *Paulusbriefe ohne Paulus?* 158–64 (cf. *Inzenierte Fälschungen*, 179–84); Van Manen, *Wave of Hypercriticism*, 81–85; Killen, "Ignatian Epistles Entirely Spurious"; among several others. However, as Lookadoo argues, the Ignatian corpus being inauthentic does not preclude us from dating it to the second century. As such, the authenticity of the Ignatian corpus is, while interesting, a footnote.

31. Knox, *Philemon Among the Letters of Paul*, 85–87.

of Knox's other suggestions have caveats (many noted by him himself).[32] For instance, Paul's greetings overlap with Ignatius', yet as noted before these also overlap with several other Pauline letters.[33] Ignatius' greeting is hardly specific to the one found in Philemon, meaning they do not provide clear evidence of Ignatius relying on Philemon in particular.[34] However, assuming Knox's suggestion that there is some kind of literary dependence, the problem becomes determining *directionality*. Notably, while Ignatius insists on the authority of Onesimus and his desire that the latter's congregation emulate him,[35] it is curious he would not reference Paul to reinforce this. However, if Philemon was composed *after* Ignatius' letter, perhaps in connection with promoting Onesimus' authority (granting him the great role of having been baptized by Paul), this would make more sense. The only letter Ignatius ever explicitly cites is 1 Corinthians.[36]

Polycarp does not mention or refer to Philemon, but he possibly uses Ephesians (though I do not consider this certain).[37] As Ephesians is known to be based on Colossians,[38] this means we can create a *terminus ad quem*

---

32. For instance, Knox, *Philemon Among the Letters of Paul*, 86.

33. Knox, *Philemon Among the Letters of Paul*, 87.

34. Contra Knox, see Martens, "Ignatius and Onesimus."

35. Ignatius, *Letter to the Ephesians* 1–6, 20.

36. Mitchell, "In the Footsteps of Paul."

37. Lookadoo, "Polycarp," 369 argues for reliance. Close analysis of Polycarp's language does not mirror Ephesians closely. For instance, the claim that the *Letter to the Philippians* 1.3 mirrors Ephesians 2:8–9 is based on two sets of three words taken out of order and spliced together: χάριτί ἐστε σεσῳσμένοι and οὐκ ἐξ ἔργων. The latter appears in other Pauline letters (Rom 9:12; Gal 2:16), Deutero-Pauline texts (Titus 3:5), and non-Pauline texts (e.g., James 2:21). While these six words appearing together raises the likelihood of this being Ephesians, we should not immediately be sold on this. I view it as tentative.

38. Scholars are generally more wary of Ephesians' authenticity. Recently, Immendörfer, *Ephesians and Artemis* contendeds that the *hapax legomena* in Ephesians can be explained as Ephesians being a genuine letter sent to Ephesus, as several of the *hapax legomena* are found in inscriptional evidence from the region. It would be hasty to conclude that this author (who was certainly aware of Ephesian traditions; see Immendörfer, *Ephesians and Artemis*, 325–26) is actually Paul. It could just as easily be a later church authority from Ephesus fabricating the letter. Immendörfer's conclusions, while tantalizing and interesting, do not uniquely point to Paul as author of the letter. We know that by the late first century, Ephesus had a thriving Christian community, and by the second century had learned bishops like "Onesimus." The letter is likewise also not attested until the middle of the second century, at the earliest. Thus, we cannot safely conclude that this was Paul writing.

for Colossians to roughly some time in the early or mid-second century.[39] However, since Philemon is not referenced and likely depends on Colossians in some way, we cannot use Polycarp as a *terminus ad quem* for Philemon. Even this date, though, would be tentative. While Irenaeus claims to have known Polycarp as a child, we cannot tell when Polycarp died, as the earliest account of his death is likely a forgery from possibly as late as the third century.[40] As such, we have no accurate idea of how we could date the *Letter to the Philippians*, save that it mentions the Ignatian letter corpus (which we also cannot date without relying on several assumptions).[41] In the third century, Origen quotes small portions of Philemon in his *Commentary on Matthew*, but not much else exists. Nothing early attests to the whole letter.

What of the manuscripts, though? These, too, are an issue. The manuscript *P Chester Beatty II* (Papyrus 46) is our oldest extant collection of Paul's letters (dating roughly to 200 per Laird[42]), but it contains no personal letters (1 and 2 Timothy, Philemon, or 2 Thessalonians for that matter). Codex Vaticanus is also missing these (and the final chapters of Hebrews), though it may have retained them originally.[43] The earliest fragment of Philemon is Papyrus 87, which is usually dated between the second and third centuries. The earliest complete copy of Philemon is Sinaiticus in the fourth century.

The verdict is not favorable to Philemon. At best, a *terminus ad quem* can only be assigned anywhere from the first century to the end of the second century, when Tertullian notes that the Marcionite canon had included it.[44] This only tells us that some form of Philemon existed at that point—we

---

39. Laird, *Pauline Corpus in Early Christianity*, 136.

40. Moss, "On the Dating of Polycarp."

41. Lookadoo, "Date and Authenticity of the Ignatian Letters," discusses these problems at length.

42. Laird, *Pauline Corpus in Early Christianity*, 319. Notably, however, these dates have been challenged; see Nongbri, *God's Library*, 145 and a date as late as the fourth century is even plausible.

43. Laird, *Pauline Corpus in Early Christianity*, 320.

44. Though some may try pushing this back further with the Muratorian Fragment (e.g., Lingelbach, *Date of the Muratorian Fragment*), I find these arguments thoroughly unconvincing. For more overview and discussion, including a decent case for a late date, see Rothschild, *Muratorian Fragment*, 191–344. For example, Lingelbach contends that the reference to Pius dates it to the second or third century, but Rothschild shows this could easily be fiction, part of the authenticating tradition that was prevalent among early Christian texts trying to grant themselves antique authority. Lingelbach likewise

cannot be certain of the letter's form or unity that far back.[45] Its status within the Marcionite canon is also problematic; Tertullian claims that Marcion did not mar the text (*Against Marcion* 5.21), while Epiphanius claims that Marcion had mutilated it, possibly implying the Marcionite version was of a different length (*Panarion* 42.12.1). Since we have no idea what it looked like in the second century, we cannot say one way or the other.

In my view, the lateness of debates on its authenticity in the early church, plus the lack in specificity on its contents, coheres with the potential inauthenticity of the letter. If it was only written during the early or middle second century, then this would explain why debates on its authenticity and utility are also late (i.e., there was no letter in wide circulation until then).[46] This likewise explains its lack of usage among Christians overtly concerned with issues of slavery during this same time. After those debates were resolved, this would further explain why some churches found it to lack utility and challenged its authorship.

Jerome clearly attests to some debate on Philemon's authenticity when discussing how critics of the letter delineate things they think Paul would never say, alongside other criticisms. Jerome finishes these thoughts by writing:

> With these and other things of this sort, they maintain either that the epistle that is written to Philemon is not Paul's; or, if it is likewise Paul's, that it contains nothing capable of edifying us; and that it was rejected by very many of the ancients, since it is written merely out of the duty to commend someone, not for teaching.[47]

---

makes a case for there being literary parallels with second- and third-century literature, but these are equally explicable if the text is late (a late text can read and utilize early texts; if the church fathers can quote older documents, so too can the Muratorian fragment). Lingelbach's work also remains unconvincing due to his lack of interaction with much current scholarship (especially German and French); the thesis is simply untenable.

45. Thus, the interpolation theories of Holtzmann, "Brief an den Philemon"; Hausrath, *History of New Testament Times*, 122–23; Brückner, *Chronologische Reihenfolge*, 200–3; and most recently, Waugh, "Philemon" cannot be summarily dismissed as they have been.

46. Fitzmyer, *Letter to Philemon*, 8; Tamez et al., *Philippians, Colossians, Philemon*, 201; Lohse, *Commentary*, 188; Williams, "'No Longer a Slave,'" 16; Decock, "Reception of the Letter to Philemon in the Early Church," 277; and Heine, "In Search of Origen's Commentary on Philemon," 120.

47. Jerome, *Commentary on Philemon*, preface. Translation from Scheck, *St. Jerome's Commentaries*, 352.

He does not specify which ancients rejected Philemon, but it is thought that part of Jerome's commentary derived from Origen's (now lost) commentary on Philemon, where he also addressed some of these critics.[48] As noted before, at least two manuscripts contain collections of Paul's letters, from which Philemon is absent, including our extant oldest collection of Paul's writings (though this might simply be in error or a result of damage).[49] Likewise, the Syrian church neglected its authenticity, as noted in the introduction.[50] All of this indicates that authenticity was not a completely settled matter regarding this letter.

Conclusions on Dating

From what can be seen above, there is no solid evidence that locates the Letter to Philemon in history. If authentic, the letter may date as early as 50 CE (per Campbell), but perhaps later if we challenge the precarious case Campbell built for dating it. Additionally, if inauthentic, it could date roughly around the same time as Paul's own life,[51] or as late as the second century. Given the dearth in references to the letter until the time of Tertullian, we can safely disregard any decisive conclusions on its dating. However, I think combining this with the letter's several peculiarities (both literary and stylistic) produces an ever so slight tilt in favor of inauthenticity and, most likely, a later date.

In what follows, I wish to propose how we might conceptualize potential motivations and reasons for fabricating such a letter, and some more contextual reasons why the letter might make more sense in a later post-Paul setting, i.e., around the second century. Taken in conjunction with the previous findings, I believe that most of these theories could push the needle toward a second-century dating for Philemon being most likely.

---

48. See Heine, "In Search of Origen's Commentary on Philemon" for discussion.

49. Walker, *Interpolations in the Pauline Letters*, 50–51n27; and Trobisch, *Paul's Letter Collection*, 20–21.

50. Tamez et al.,, *Philippians, Colossians, Philemon*, 201; Lohse, *Commentary*, 188; Williams, "'No Longer a Slave,'" 16.

51. 2 Thess 3:17 seems to indicate such issues were already prevalent in early Pauline circles.

MOTIVATIONS FOR FORGERY

In what follows, I will provide five possible explanations for why someone might have forged Philemon. Some of these are not as compatible with each other as others, though one could possibly jam them together and form a single super-theory of forged origins.

(1) The Letter as Christian-Stoic Commentary and Instruction

As far back as the works of Bruno Bauer, scholars have recognized that Stoicism and early Christianity movements overlapped, both in the broad scope of their ideas and on the minutiae of many positions.[52] While it was once customary to refer to Philemon's emancipatory brilliance, more recent studies from Green and others (noted above) reveal that, in truth, this letter is not revolutionary. Generally, the language of "Paul" in Philemon is not to be considered unique even with the apparent attempt at humanizing slaves. Referring to a slave as a "brother," spiritually or fraternally, is not akin to ascribing him equality with his master, nor is it unheard of in Roman literature. In his *Diatribe*, Epictetus describes the slave and his brethren born of Zeus as fundamentally the same in nature, creating distance from the Aristotelian idea that slaves had innate inclinations toward being slaves. This was a particular trait of Stoic philosophy; Seneca advocated for high treatment of slaves, including dining with them and beyond.[53] Epictetus says (*Discourse* 1.13):

> Now when someone asked him how it is possible to eat acceptably to the gods, he said, If it is done justly and graciously and fairly and restrainedly and decently, is it not also done acceptably to the gods? And when you have asked for warm water and the slave does not heed you; or if he does heed you but brings in tepid water; or if he is not even to be found in the house, then to refrain from anger and not to explode, is not this acceptable to the gods?—How, then, can a man bear with such persons?—Slave, will you not bear with your own brother, who has Zeus as his progenitor and is, as it were, a son born of the same seed as yourself and

---

52. Bauer, *Christ and the Caesars*; Van den Bergh van Eysinga, "Christelijke Denkbeelden bij Seneca"; Rasimus, Engberg-Pedersen, and Dunderberg, eds., *Stoicism in Early Christianity*, among several others.

53. Epictetus, *Diatribe* 1.13 regards all people as kin, as we are all descendants of Zeus; see Aune, "Problem of Equality in the Church and Society," 173.

of the same sowing from above; but if you have been stationed in a like position above others, will you forthwith set yourself up as a tyrant? Do you not remember that you are, and over whom you rule—that they are kinsmen, that they are brothers by nature, that they are offspring of Zeus?—But I have a deed of sale for them, and they have none for me.—Do you see whither you bend your gaze, that it is to the earth, that it is to the pit, that it is to these wretched laws of ours, the laws of the dead, and that it is not to the laws of the gods that you look?[54]

We can see here parallels with the Letter to Philemon, where Aune points out that Philemon and Onesimus are one in Christ.[55] Here, the deity unites them as kin, and Epictetus further encourages patience and non-anger as the answer to disobedient and absent slaves, both of which parallel our situation in Philemon. Just compare this with Philemon 15–16:

Perhaps because of this he was separated from you for a time so that you might have him eternally, no longer as a slave but greater than a slave, a beloved brother. He is very precious to me especially, however how much more to you, both in the flesh and in the Lord.[56]

The parallels are rather obvious. "Paul" implores that Philemon receive Onesimus not just as a slave, but as a human with the same divine kinship as he. This, essentially, is a reversal of what we see above in the *Diatribe* by Epictetus, where the slave is implored not to elevate himself above his brethren and to instead see they are brothers with a shared kinship in Zeus. Philemon being emancipatory text is not evidenced by the text (nor any ancient Christian commentaries on it). Ancient Christians and pagans notably did not see a need to challenge the existence of slavery as an institution, although there was debate about their treatment and general fraternity with others.[57] Stoic parallels do not end here; Seneca himself in his noteworthy *Epistle* 42 writes:

I am glad to learn, through those who come from you, that you live on friendly terms with your slaves. This befits a sensible and well-educated man like yourself. "They are slaves," people declare. Nay, rather they are men. "Slaves!" No, comrades. "Slaves!" No, they are

54. Translation from Epictetus, *Discourses Books 1–2*, 97–99.
55. Aune, "Problem of Equality in the Church and Society," 173–74.
56. Translation mine.
57. Aune, "Problem of Equality in the Church and Society," 169–75.

unpretentious friends. "Slaves!" No, they are our fellow-slaves, if
one reflects that Fortune has equal rights over slaves and free men
alike. That is why I smile at those who think it degrading for a man
to dine with his slave. But why should they think it degrading?[58]

Indeed, it is no wonder that early Christians developed a fond relationship with Stoics, especially Seneca, who was included in lists of Christian authors.[59] This continued coalescing in relation to Paul. In the third or
fourth century a set of personal letters (much like Philemon) were forged
depicting a correspondence between Seneca and Paul. Tertullian himself lays claims to Seneca, referring to him as "one of ours" (*Seneca saepe
noster*).[60] It is also evident that the Stoic conception of the slave as a brother
with divine unity in Zeus took explicit shape by the middle first century
and the end of the second century. Thus, by the end of the second century,
Christians were already attempting to claim the works of Seneca.

It is not hard to detect that from the later first or second century and
onward, Christians were becoming more familiar with the teachings of
the Stoics and, consequently, developing literature that incorporated and
appropriated Stoic ideas and personalities. Specifically, the forged letters
between Paul and Seneca provide, in my view, a prime context for the development of Philemon. But why specifically would this letter have been
invented?

If we argued this was a Christian forgery attempting to bring Stoic
principles into play, and further considered the relationship that Philemon
appears to have with Colossians-Ephesians, one could argue that Philemon
is an expansion and commentary on passages in those other letters (Col
3:22–4:1; Eph 6:5–9) concerning slavery and the slave-master relationship.
This has been previously argued by Baur, Steck, Van Manen, and Schwab.[61]
As Steck observed, "Almost the whole epistle to Philemon can be derived
from other Pauline epistles in form and content."[62] Schwab further notes
that in Col 3:11, the author conveys there are to be no distinctions in Christ

58. Translation from Seneca, *Epistles 1–65*, 301–3.

59. Jerome, *Ecclesiastici Scriptores* includes Seneca based on the exchanged letters
between he and Paul (forgeries).

60. Tertullian, *Treatise on the Soul* 20.

61. Baur, *Paul*, 305–8; Steck, "Plinius im Neuen Testament"; Van Manen, *Wave of
Hypercriticism*, 150; Schwab, *Echtheitskritische Untersuchungen zu den vier kleineren
Paulusbriefen*, 156–57.

62. Steck, "Plinius im Neuen Testament," 576. Translation mine.

on account of social differences, but then in 3:22—4:1 these differences manifest when conducting slave-master relations. Philemon, as a result, would be an attempt at clarifying the tension of these passages.

The circumstances of Onesimus' wronging of Philemon are, in this case, immaterial. Instead, a Christian reader would be able to insert whatever grievance they had and see in the letter an instruction for how to engage their own slaves via Paul entreating Philemon. In this case, regardless of the crime, they are to see their slaves as siblings in Christ, make amends, and take them back into their service. However, using Paul as a stand-in for the church, it seems that the slave might instead be dedicated into service; i.e., if the slave owner found the slave's misdeeds to be too egregious, they could turn the slave over to other Christians or the church itself for other uses. The name Onesimus, lifted from Colossians, would serve as a perfect name here for a slave, allowing the puns and general allegory of the tale.[63]

Notably, while "Paul" places an onus on Philemon (and thereby Christian slave owners as a whole) to treat their slaves as brothers in Christ, the onus still largely rests on slaves to do the manual work of repair, i.e., to be the "useful" individuals. Onesimus will, as a pun on his name, be useful (εὔχρηστον) to Philemon again (Phlm 11), and that lingers in the background.[64] This references slaves having the onus to behave well and execute the will of their masters (Col 3:22—4:1), as Knapp discusses.[65] The letter, as a result, primarily serves to instruct the Christian slave-owning class on how to better manage their slaves, pulling from Stoic philosophy and teachings on the matter.

In this way, Philemon gives practical instruction for implementing what is written in Colossians for wider Christian interests. The idea that Philemon entered the canon alone, and without Colossians in particular, seems unlikely.[66] Given the letter was contentious specifically due to its lack of utility among early Christians, it is likely that the letter's attribution to Paul's and relationship to Colossians is what saved it from fading into obscurity. We can consider the relationship between these letters as interdependent, as noted in chapter 3. In this case, what it is that Onesimus

63. Von Weizsäcker, *Apostolic Age of the Church*, 244–45. The name Apphia was another known in the region of Colossae; see Huttner, *Early Christianity in the Lycus Valley*, 85.

64. Note, that this "usefulness" may also entail more sinister implications, specifically of the sexual utility of Onesimus; see Marchal, "Usefulness of an Onesimus."

65. Knapp, *Invisible Romans*, 136.

66. Johnson, *Constructing Paul*, 247–71.

did and the issue of whether Onesimus is being set free are entirely inconsequential issues when reading Philemon as a commentary on Colossians. While some, like Jennifer Glancy in her latest edition of *Slavery in Early Christianity* (2024), contend that the ambiguity of Philemon makes it a "futile" starting point for understanding early Christian attitudes toward slavery,[67] ambiguity may in fact be the entire point of the letter (if read as a forgery). It is not about any specific misdeed that Onesimus has committed.[68] Instead, it is about the management and reconciliation process for Christian slave owners. Onesimus' status as a slave is permanent and unchanging (manumission was arguably not an available option to consider), and his misdeed could be *anything*. They are projectable details by the reader. Thus, the letter might have been forged as a standard instructional manual on how to treat slaves in a case of their general wrongdoing or a rift forming between master and slave, whatever that might be. The letter, then, presents two options: (1) ensure the Christian background of the slave and take them back into one's service; or (2) they could be given to other Christians, particularly leaders (like Paul), for other uses (Phlm 13–14[69]). In this case, the letter contextually best fits with later issues in Christianity: determining how to treat slaves, and their growing interest in Stoicism in the second century. As time went on and the institution of slavery was taken for granted within Christianity (as well as Christian treatment of slaves), Philemon's utility faded until later scribes were at a loss for what to do with it.

(2) The Letter as a Pseudo-Plinian Forgery

Steck's theory, which is admittedly eccentric, argues that the Letter to Philemon is really a clever Christian rewrite of Pliny's letter to Sabinianus.[70] Pliny writes:

---

67. Glancy, *Slavery in Early Christianity* (2024), 136–37.

68. This addresses the issues of trying to reconstruct the historical and theological background as well; see Brogdon, *Companion to Philemon*. Ultimately, it is a piece of literature from a slave-owning class.

69. Here Paul desires to keep Onesimus, but only with the consent of Philemon. Otherwise, Onesimus will return to Philemon's service as a "useful" work body.

70. Steck, "Plinius im Neuen Testament," 570–84; Van Manen, *Wave of Hypercriticism*, 149.

Your freedman with whom you said you were angry has been with me; he threw himself at my feet and clung to me with as much submission as he could have done at yours. He earnestly requested me with many tears, and even with all the eloquence of silent sorrow, to intercede for him; in short, he convinced me by his whole behavior, that he sincerely repents of his fault. And I am persuaded he is thoroughly reformed, because he knows that he was wrong. / I know you are angry with him, and I know too, it is not without reason; but mercy is never more worthy of praise than when there is the justest cause for anger. You once loved this man, and, I hope, will again: in the meanwhile, let me only prevail with you to pardon him. If he should incur your displeasure hereafter, you will have so much the stronger reason for your anger, as you show yourself willing to forgive him now. Allow something in his youth, to his tears, and to your own gentle disposition: do not make him uneasy any longer, and I will add too, do not make yourself so; for a man of your kindness of heart cannot be angry without feeling great uneasiness. / I am afraid that if I add my prayers to his, I would seem to be compelling you rather than asking you to forgive him. Yet I will do it and in the strongest terms since I have rebuked him very sharply and severely, warning him that I will never intercede for him again. Although it was proper to say this to him, in order to frighten him, it was not intended for your hearing. I may possibly have the occasion to again intercede for him and obtain your forgiveness if the error is one which is suitable for my intercession and your pardon.[71]

Another letter worth mentioning is Pliny's follow-up with Sabinianus (*Ep.* 9.24), which Steck likewise finds relevant to the origins of Philemon. This will be discussed later in the book.

The parallels, of course, are clear between these letters, and it is no wonder that Pliny's are often read in conjunction with Philemon,[72] though this practice certainly has its detractors.[73] Dissimilarities, too, are immediate. Onesimus is enslaved while Sabinianus' grievances are with a freedman. Pliny affirms Sabinianus' anger and frustration toward his freedman, whereas Paul seems to divert Philemon's ire. Conversely, Pliny asks

71. Stowers, *Letter Writing in Greco-Roman Antiquity*, 160.

72. As McKnight, *Letter to Philemon*, 42 notes, Pliny's letter is "Discussed in almost every study of Philemon . . ."

73. Fitzmyer, *Letter to Philemon*, 20–23; Ip, *Socio-Rhetorical Interpretation*, 7–9; Knox, *Philemon Among the Letters of Paul*, 16–18; Seesengood, *Philemon*, 61–62; Callahan, *Embassy of Onesimus*, 7–8 among several others.

Sabinianus to forgive his freedman, whereas Paul merely offers to repay damages. Differences are certainly there. On the other hand, we might reply that some differences are far less noteworthy than they first appear; being a slave and being a freedman often entailed many of the same responsibilities, and because freedmen often gained little in terms of social status,[74] the two are more similar in their social stations than dissimilar.[75]

Eduard Lohse has compared Pliny's letters to Philemon, and a point he makes, in the interest of distinguishing the letters, is that Pliny appeals to Sabinianus from the standpoint of a Stoic, whereas Paul's perspective is more Christian. He writes:

> Paul also intercedes for a runaway slave. He, however, does not say that the master should exercise the Stoic virtue of clemency and show himself to be mild-mannered. Rather, Paul speaks to him in terms of Christian love and faith. The apostle weights his words carefully and fashions the structure of the principal part of the letter in such a way that the addressee is gradually led to the actual request.[76]

But upon closer inspection, Philemon does appear to be influenced by Stoic thought. Attempting to garner Philemon's love and sympathy for Onesimus due to their shared divine heritage closely parallels the words of Epictetus (*Discourse* 1.13). Given this, Lohse inadvertently provides another point of comparison between Pliny's letters and Philemon: both are personal letters dealing with master-subordinate relations and reconciliation, and both appeal in particularly Stoic fashion.

By contrast, the similarities are great and often specific. Paul and Pliny both wish not to give the impression they are compelling their targets (Phlm 8, 14, cf. *Ep.* 9.21.4, *vereor ne videar non rogare sed cogere*). Despite this, both explicitly offer their prayers (Phlm 4–7, cf. *Ep.* 9.21.4, *si precibus eius meas iunxero*), and both appeal for leniency by citing the master's love for the party seeking intercession (Phlm 9, cf. *Ep.* 9.21.3, *Amasti hominem et*). In Paul's case, he uses his own status to appeal for leniency as well. Neither Pliny nor Paul clearly seeks manumission,[77] and both are willing to

74. Steck, "Plinius im Neuen Testament," 578–79; Pao, *Colossians & Philemon*, 350.

75. Steck, "Plinius im Neuen Testament," 578–79 anticipated this very contention raised by modern critics.

76. Lohse, *Colossians and Philemon*, 197–98.

77. Pliny clearly cares little about whether the freedman gains true freedom from his master. As Green notes regarding Philemon, "Nothing here compels us to the view that

take charges of anger and dissuade them. Paul says he would take upon any charges owed by Onesimus (Phlm 18–19), while Pliny says that he would again intercede on behalf of the freedman if necessary (*Ep.* 9.21.4).

Following this, Steck contends that the author of Philemon is looking at the letter from Pliny to Sabinianus and altering key components to create a Christocentric version. Instead of "pure humanity" being the philosophical underpinning of this plea, it is instead "Christian faith and Christian charity." Steck's thesis advocates almost an admixture, wherein the letter clearly derives much of its contents and theological affects from other Pauline letters (principally 1 Corinthians, Colossians, and Ephesians) while its story comes primarily from Pliny's letter. As evidence of this, Steck ushers a number of passages he thinks evinces Pliny's style from Latin to Greek translation, such as the following:

Phlm 8	Pliny, *Ep.* 9.21.4	Pliny, *Ep.* 9.24
Διὸ πολλὴν ἐν Χριστῷ παρρησίαν ἔχων ἐπιτάσσειν σοι τὸ ἀνῆκον	vereor ne videor non rogare, sed cogere	quod tantum mihi tribuis, ut vel auctoritati meae pareas, vel precibus indulgeas

Here, Steck observes that the shift between using his apostolic authority and personal intimacy is paralleled in Pliny's own shifts in using authority vs. friendship. Likewise, Steck finds parallels in various other passages.[78] That Pliny influenced the New Testament is hardly a theory isolated to Steck either, with Mark G. Bilby recently arguing similarly for the Acts of the Apostles.[79]

We could combine this theory with the previous one; in an attempt to create a commentary instructing Christian masters on the proper treatment and reception of slaves who have committed some misdeed, the forger took as their model the letters of Pliny to Sabinianus. This, of course, is not

Onesimus's [case] meets eligibility for formal manumission under Roman law, nor that informal manumission to an underclass status is being advocated" (see Green, "Paul's Letter to Philemon," 104). Cf. Paley, "Questioning the Pauline Authorship of Philemon," 13, who thinks the issue is simply too vague to tell what the author of Philemon intended regarding manumission.

78. Phlm 16, cf. Pliny, *Ep.* 9.24 (*bene fecisti quod libertum aliquando tibi carum reducentibus epistulis meis in domum in animum recepisti*); Phlm 22, cf. Pliny, *Ep.* 9.24 (*simul in posterum moneo, ut te erroribus tuorum, etsi non fuerit qui deprecetur, placabilem praestes*). See Steck, "Plinius im Neuen Testament," 580.

79. Bilby, "Pliny's Correspondence and the Acts of the Apostles."

entirely out of the question. Early Christians were familiar with Pliny,[80] making this theory at least possible; the first figure to mention the existence of Philemon, Tertullian, also used Pliny's letter collection when discussing the early history of Christian persecution.[81] The motivation behind overtly Christianizing these Roman letters—which, on their surface, are already amenable to such Christianization—would be utilizing the noble Pliny to promote a general treatment of slaves who have done their Christian masters wrong. In short, the forgery is instructional and specifically written using Paul's name to grant it particular authority.

(3) The Letter as Apostolic Succession Fiction

The next theory I will discuss (but surely not the final way of contemplating Philemon as a forgery) argues that the letter, far from being a commentary or how-to guide, is instead a sociopolitically motivated piece. Argued, to my knowledge, first by Stephan Huller and then by Robert M. Price, this theory advocates that there is, indeed, a strong connection between the bishop Onesimus mentioned in Ignatius' *Epistle to the Ephesians* and the Letter to Philemon, and further that Philemon was a forgery meant to validate bishop Onesimus' position and authority.[82] That the letter was meant to codify apostolic and later church authority has been further argued by Schwab, who postulated that it could function as extended commentary on Colossians.[83] To expand on this, it is necessary to see how Philemon would function in this way (particularly with Colossians) by comparing directly with Ignatius' letter.

Ignatius seems to be attempting to get a particular congregation to adhere to the authority of Onesimus. Ignatius' *Letter to the Ephesians* 1.3 states:

> Since, then, I have received your entire congregation in the name of God through Onesimus, who abides in a love that defies description and serves as your bishop in the flesh—and I ask by Jesus Christ that you love him, and that all of you be like him. For

80. Corke-Webster, "Early Reception of Pliny the Younger."

81. Tertullian, *Apologeticum* 2.

82. Price, *Amazing Colossal Apostle*, 503–4.

83. Schwab, *Echtheitskritische Untersuchungen zu den vier kleineren Paulusbriefen*, 152–57.

blessed is the one who has graciously granted you, who are worthy, to obtain such a bishop.[84]

Ignatius continues (*Letter to the Ephesians* 6):

The more one notices that the bishop is silent, the more he should stand in awe of him. For we must receive everyone that the master of the house sends to take care of his affairs as if he were the sender himself. And so we are clearly obliged to look upon the bishop as the Lord himself. Thus Onesimus himself praises you highly for being so well ordered in God, because all of you live according to the truth and no heresy resides among you. On the contrary, you no longer listen to anyone, except one who speaks truthfully about Jesus Christ.[85]

We see there is a clear concern with the bishop's authority; that the congregation is instructed specifically to be thankful and in awe of Onesimus may indicate some contention over Onesimus' leadership. As such, in the second century, this bishop Onesimus had a need for authorization, which Ignatius attempted to provide. This gives a potential basis for forgery. Even if there was no obvious challenge to his authority, the second century was a time when the church was actively concerned with its bishops and leaders establishing apostolic descent (discussed below). Thus, the authority of Onesimus would surely come up. How is it then resolved?

Enter the Epistles to Philemon and Colossians. To reiterate a bit of discussion from chapter 2, Philemon's text uses Paul's imprisonment not to realistically portray prison life, but to place him at a similar station to Onesimus, going so far (Phlm 13) as to suggest that Paul would like him as an aid in missionary work while the apostle is in chains. This grants Onesimus the slave a great deal of authority as an emissary of Paul, which is borne out further by his role in Paul's itinerant mission in Col 4:9. Were Philemon a forgery meant to boost the bishop Onesimus' reputation, then multiple details in it become clearer, including the fact that Paul is never referred to as an apostle and is instead given the title "prisoner" (distinct from every other epistle).

Disclosing the humble origins of a great figure is commonplace in Greco-Roman tales; Philemon certainly gives the bishop Onesimus a far more relatable and laudable background, having gone from slave to bishop—a perfect analogy for the freedom in Christ that Paul speaks of

84. Ignatius in Ehrman, *Apostolic Fathers*, 221.
85. Ignatius in Ehrman, *Apostolic Fathers*, 225–27.

in 1 Cor 7:21–24. This theory is consistent with theory (1) as well, as it could be a suitable companion and practical commentary to Colossians and Ephesians. It thus gains multiple uses for a potential forger.

Contextually, it also makes some amount of sense. Certainly, by the second century, church fathers regularly enshrined their authority via apostolic succession stories. This can be seen particularly in the works of Irenaeus and Tertullian, who utilize apostolic succession to validate church fathers they either regarded as authoritative or had direct connections with. Irenaeus, for example, wishes to authorize his mentor Polycarp's authority by connecting him with the apostle John (*apud* Jerome, *Chronicon* under entry for the 219th Olympiad; cf. Tertullian, *Against Heretics* 32). Infamously, however, Irenaeus combines different Johns in his writing, indicating that he has no firsthand knowledge and has instead invented an apostolic lineage.[86] Others receive apostolic lineages to promote their authoritative positions as well.[87]

The letters to the Colossians and to Philemon together could promote the bishop Onesimus as (A) having a traditionally Greco-Roman life narrative of coming from humble origins to leadership, which (B) parallels calls for the Christian to be a slave of Christ (with his literal slavery) and (C) demonstrates Onesimus' direct connections to the apostle Paul, granting him authority by association. As with Polycarp, we have here an invented lineage from Paul to Onesimus. This would further necessitate a roughly second-century date for the Letter to Philemon, as it would have to be contextually associated with the conditions that bishop Onesimus faced in his congregation around the time Ignatius was writing.

(4) Philemon and Colossians as Legitimacy Assertion

One theory may present us with another interesting possibility. In the Acts of the Apostles, Paul's travels are all relayed in some detail to us, emphasizing his journey and experiences up until very near his death. Acts appears to be hinting at his impending doom.[88] The noticeable problem is that all the way up until that point, Paul is never described as traveling to or having

---

86. Kok, *Beloved Apostle?* 58–102.

87. Tertullian, *Against Heretics* 32 has several listed. See also Irenaeus, *Against Heresies* 3.3.2–3.

88. Fitzmyer, *Acts of the Apostles*, 55.

any association with Colossae.[89] In fact, Colossae is noticeably absent from ancient discourse on Paul throughout the first and early second centuries.[90] Despite this, we know that by the end of the second century, a church had sprung up in Colossae. The Letter to the Colossians is mentioned by Tertullian and by Irenaeus and was apparently a part of Marcion's *Apostolikon* by the end of the second century, when Tertullian had a copy of it. Christians in Colossae were evidently so small and unremarkable that most writers simply did not acknowledge them.

Given their small presence, their being ignored by most other Christians, one argument in favor of Philemon and Colossians being paired forgeries would be to promote and edify the Colossian Christian communities in the second century, bringing them into fuller accord and recognition with other churches. Giving themselves Pauline authority and apostolic succession, as a result, would be of immense importance in this regard. This would, in turn, coalesce with other theories mentioned above.

The Amoral Forgery

In his recent publication in *Early Christianity*, Isaac T. Soon discusses at length the amoral nature of some early Christian forgery, which could apply to Philemon.[91] The church father Salvian forged letters in Timothy's name, and we are lucky enough to have a separate letter discussing his motivations for doing so.[92] Salvian provides possibly the best case, as he not only forges writing in Timothy's name, but mimics other Pauline epistles with Timothy's name attached to recreate the style.[93] Soon writes:

> Among the reasons Salvian gives for writing in Timothy's name are that people in his day often read things because of an author's reputation rather than the content itself and that the author is a humble person who does not claim attention for himself, avoiding vanity in pursuit of heavenly rewards.[94]

---

89. Eurell, "Second Imprisonment of Paul," 234.

90. I can find no overt mention of Colossae in any Christian writings until past Justin Martyr.

91. Soon, "Before Deception."

92. Salvian, *Ep.* 9.

93. Soon, "Before Deception," 435–36.

94. Soon, "Before Deception," 437.

If any of the above arguments for forgery are correct, they could also explain why a forger might write a letter to Philemon in Paul's hand. Whether as Christian instruction or as a more overt attempt to justify a bishop's station, the forger may have chosen Paul's name not merely to deceive people but to (A) emphasize the importance of the topic for which they were forging and (B) humble themselves by removing their own name from the equation. Forgery was not always an overtly deceptive act; sometimes it was borne from Christian humility or awe, as was the case with the *Acts of Paul*. However, below I propose one more reason for forgery that further challenges how we should characterize or moralize ancient forgery.

(5) Philemon as Slave Necessity

In her recent book *God's Ghostwriters* (2024), Candida Moss discusses at length the usage of slaves as scribes and essentially ghostwriters by early Christians. Paul himself utilized slaves extensively throughout the production of his own literature. The Letter to the Romans is a key example of this, where the slave Tertius was surely the scribe (and probably more).[95] One suggestion that likewise caught my attention in this volume was that Onesimus was perhaps the scribe behind the Letter to Philemon.[96]

Perhaps there is some reason to suppose that Onesimus may be more than the scribe, in this case. The letter itself shows potential evidence of being composed from previous Pauline letters, as noted in chapter 3. It likewise demonstrates little to no awareness or care for scriptural references, nor does it incorporate an overtly complicated degree of theology. If Onesimus, a literate slave, were in a tight spot, perhaps composing a letter to Philemon utilizing Paul's authority would be particularly helpful for him. In this case, he might have taken an authentic (or inauthentic) letter like Colossians and used this as his base for Paul's general style. The Letter to Colossians itself attests to a desire for it to be put into circulation (4:16). As such, he would have also had the opportunity to peruse it.

Thus, it could also be that this was a slave letter of desperation. An attempt at reconciliation where none otherwise may have been available. Onesimus' suggestion that he would be a good brother in Christ and a "useful" one could evince the weight of this desperate act, as the Greek

95. Moss, *God's Ghostwriters*, 58.
96. Moss, *God's Ghostwriters*, 58.

εὔχρηστος (Phlm 11) is often a double entendre for sexual favor or exploitation.[97] In this case, Onesimus, a slave hoping to be reconciled and avoid the stern punishments that Roman law would inflict upon him (even possible death), may have composed the letter in a last bid for assistance, offering up his entire body and personhood to make it happen.[98] Paul may have even signed off on the piece, but contributed little to nothing that warrants deeming him an author in any capacity. The letter's shape, style, and composition might all be from Onesimus, with Paul being ascribed credit for it, as was typical of the time. In this sense, I would still consider it an un-Pauline epistle. Instead, it would be the single surviving "Onesimusine" epistle.

THE OBJECTION FROM INNOCUOUSNESS

One of the most common (and probably strongest) defenses that has ever been offered in favor of Philemon is that the epistle is just so innocuous that it baffles one to imagine its invention. As seen above, though, we can posit numerous reasons for forging such an epistle and the functions it could then serve. The response, of course, would be to contend that such propositions are not enough to warrant it being a forgery. There would need to be more.[99]

But the question, ultimately, is why? We have certainly seen letters forged with far less apparent purpose, sometimes presenting little more than brief fictions. The fabricated corpus of Apollonian letters "collected" by Philostratus is a prime example. Forging sources and stories of how those sources came into existence was, in fact, a rather common authorization strategy in antiquity, making fabricated/fictional letter writing

---

97. Marchal, "Usefulness of an Onesimus."

98. A response to this theory may be that as Onesimus forges Paul's offer to repay Onesimus' damages or owed debts, that this indicates Paul must have had a hand in authorizing the letter. However, this may not be the case. As is infamously said, it is better to ask for forgiveness than permission. Onesimus may have, again, been reaching in desperation.

99. There is of course one other retort: "I am simply not convinced by these explanations." This presents no fundamental challenge either; since we can easily see reasons for forgery, there were likely other reasons such a letter could be forged. That these explanations are unconvincing does not mean there was not one in the past that we have now lost. Thus, those arguing *for* authenticity likewise have an onus to show why it would *not* be a forgery as well.

widespread.[100] We have seen forgeries for polemical purposes, as mere exercises in imitation, for theological reasons, as counternarratives, as authorization strategies, etc. In short, we have seen ancient authors fabricate letters for just about every purpose imaginable; to claim that none of these explanations are enough seems like pleading for Philemon to be exceptional.

Perhaps its innocuousness is what makes it the perfect forgery. However, as noted above, there are several reasons to think this letter is far more conspicuous than most scholars are willing to admit. The letter being forged as an instructional commentary on slavery and management for the Christian slave-owning class, in fact, would be one excellent reason to create such a letter; as such a class began to expand, the need arose to address these issues in the late first and second centuries onward. Forgeries can (and do) take all shapes and sizes, and serve all manners of purpose.

FINAL THOUGHTS ON FORGERY

Was Philemon written in the second century, and can we guess the purpose of its forgery? The answers are hardly definitive, but we can tentatively say yes to each of these, were one convinced by the evidence put forward. Of course, most academics will not be convinced by these arguments or potential reasons for forgery, which is fine. The primary purpose of this chapter is, itself, hypothetical. We can see that Philemon, based on the available evidence, can fit within a second-century context just as well as it can within a first-century context, and in some ways I would even say that the former is the better fit. With that in mind, along with the fact that it is quite possible to see why this letter would be forged (perhaps multiple intersecting reasons why), we can see that basically no arguments raised in favor of authenticity stand up to scrutiny. It is not that those proclaiming the secure authenticity of Philemon actually have convincing argumentation to back this up—it is that they are unwilling to delve into the issue themselves, making the assumption of authenticity so commonplace that to suggest otherwise is practically insulting.

In this chapter, we demonstrated that, yes, this tiny and innocuous letter could have been forged with clear intent. Did that happen? We may never know for certain, but when combining all evidence laid out over the

---

100. See Rosenmeyer, *Ancient Greek Literary Letters*; Costa, *Greek Fictional Letters*; Trapp, *Greek and Latin Letters*, 27–33.

course of this volume, I would have to say that forgery is quite possible. Of all the theories above, I personally favor (1) the most and (3) second, and the two could easily be intermixed in intents. But regardless of this or whether anyone is convinced by my work here, I believe that the ball is now in the court of those arguing for authenticity: provide a detailed and worthwhile case for why Philemon ought to be considered an authentically Pauline epistle.

Afterword

FOR A LETTER AMOUNTING to only a few hundred words (less than the number it takes to fill a single 11x8.5-inch page with single-spaced, 12-point Times New Roman font), it is amazing just how much material and musing can come out of Philemon. Most people who read the New Testament could pass over the entire epistle just by accidentally folding two or three pages of their Bible's thin paper, blinking it away like an eyelash would dust. And yet, I have managed to produce tens of thousands of words questioning the very authenticity of this otherwise inconspicuous letter. Some may ask: why?

For me, the answer is both complex and simple. Pauline studies have been obsessed with the question of authenticity since its inception. Spurred on by the desire for an "authentic" or "real" Paul, and to reconstruct his life, teachings, and theology (namely with apologetic doctrinal aims in mind), many Pauline scholars have sought to find the maximal Paul possible and, as a result, have developed an unchallenged core of letters. Why are they unchallenged? It is not because there is nothing worth challenging; as seen above, contra Knox and others who wax poetic about how Philemon "bears in itself every mark of genuineness,"[1] the reality is far different.

Perhaps part of the problem is that many (if not most) studies on Philemon up to this point have come from more confessional spheres of influence, which historically have a vested interest in the authenticity of Paul's letters; authenticity and authority often comingle. As Mark Letteney writes, "The notion that textual authority derives from the identity of the author is so commonplace that we have forgotten a time where any other paradigm reigned."[2] However, as is becoming more frequently understood

1. Knox, *Philemon Among the Letters of Paul*, 28.
2. Letteney, "Authenticity and Authority," 33.

among academics, this is not a historically borne out assumption. Isaac T. Soon's work demonstrates that a text being forged did not automatically strip it of sacred authority, nor did it indicate an inherent dishonesty or fraudulent character in the author.[3] Forgeries were often noble in intent and received as authoritative despite being forged. Likewise, a text being regarded as authentic does not grant it authority, as the case of Philemon demonstrates; some early Christians regarded it as trivial and lacking in utility, thus having no authority (assuming Paul wrote it). We cannot, in fact, treat these two concepts as identical, as much as scholars (and laity) have previously assumed them to be. In this volume I am not, in any way, impugning the scriptural authority of Philemon—I am simply asking a historical question of it.

Despite the evidence that such concepts are not codependent, it has been readily assumed. As a result, I think this has created some unconscious desire to protect the Pauline corpus from scrutiny. We can certainly see twinges of this discomfort arising in chapter 1 with examples like F. F. Bruce and Joseph A. Fitzmyer, which leads them to make completely indefensible claims. Philemon does not, in fact, bear all the hallmarks of an ostensibly Pauline letter. Either we need to be more stringent in how we define something as "Pauline" (thus excluding Philemon, Colossians, and Ephesians) or we should be more open so that our corpus expands to include them.

MY FINDINGS

One issue I wished to showcase is the inconsistent manner in which scholars have addressed inauthenticity. The letter has a rather small sample size, which means that scholars have broadly dismissed stylistic arguments against its authenticity. Meanwhile, as Paley notes, the Pastoral Epistles that also have rather small sample sizes are routinely argued to be inauthentic based on style.[4] Additionally, they have simply ignored the glaring problem with making claims about sample size: if the sample size is too small to argue for inauthenticity, it is likewise too small to argue for authenticity. Assuming, however, the sample sizes are enough, there are several reasons to have doubts about this small letter's authenticity (including several *hapax*

---

3. Soon, "Before Deception."
4. Paley, "Questioning the Pauline Authorship of Philemon," 17–20.

legomena, its correlations with other letters of suspect origin, and possible copying from previous letters).

I have raised additional potential issues. This letter seems to have relationships with other letters, potentially copying from 1 Corinthians and Philippians and resembling Colossians and Ephesians. The idea of Paul copying his letters while sitting in a prison cell, again, strains credulity. If we assume Philippians authentic, following Verhoef and the vast majority of scholars, we see noteworthy differences. Philippians is veiled, at times seeming to hide or protect fellow Christians, which suggests that Paul is truly in prison and worried about the harm that could come to those he names. Meanwhile, Philemon openly names everyone associated with him. Philippians utilizes euphemism for Paul's imprisonment. Philemon states it outright. Notably, this overt interest in Paul's imprisonment largely starts in the late first and second centuries, which includes forging several letters in Paul's name. Curiously, Paul shows virtually no interest in issues related to master-slave relationships within each of the other undisputed Pauline letters, suggesting they were not pertinent. Only at the point where slave-owners were joining Christian movements en masse would slavery have been a noticeable problem that warranted response. With this in mind, I presented a number of hypotheses for fabricating this letter, some being proffered in the past and some being my own. The letter bears the hallmarks of Stoic influence, both in its language and description of slaves as kin of their owners, as well as being united in the body of Christ (just as Stoics believed slaves and their owners were all kin through Zeus).

Some may (probably will) react to this volume by insisting that many of these features or obscurities may be the result of a secretary or cowriter, but my response would be: if this work is so much the product of a secretary or cowriter that it makes little sense in the name of Paul, why would we refer to it as one of Paul's letters? This seems to obscure this letter's production behind the name of someone who was not its creator, who may have merely applied his name and taken credit for the work of others. Are we not obscuring their labor and creative roles simply to affirm Pauline authenticity? In my view, there is little way to salvage the authenticity of this letter. We would not (or should not) consider a ghostwritten novel to be the intellectual and creative genius of someone who merely took credit for others' labor. Why we should do so for Paul, other than out of a desire to save Pauline authenticity from scrutiny, escapes me.

This, of course, has immense ramifications. Without the authenticity of Philemon, we are far more justified in challenging the authenticity of Colossians and Ephesians, which has historically been tied to Philemon.[5] And this is just the start. This little letter carries a lot of weight in Pauline studies, despite its neglect relative to Paul's larger and more "substantial" works. What are we to do with a Paul-less Philemon? That is beyond the scope of this work, but perhaps the answer is simple: many creative and imaginative things.

All of this might (and likely would) be rebutted intensely by scholars wishing to maintain the authenticity of the Letter to Philemon. However, here is where I must bring up the final issue of this volume: the burden of proof. All who make *any* claim carry a burden of proof.[6] If one asserts inauthenticity, they have a burden to affirm that assertion, just as those who assert authenticity must affirm theirs. This creates a complicated scenario. Simply debunking the arguments of those promoting inauthenticity is not necessarily an argument for authenticity. There is, in fact, a third position: if one cannot provide satisfactory argumentation that favors either side, we must conclude that we cannot decide who wrote this letter. Arguing against the opposition is not an argument for one's own side—it could instead be an argument for agnosticism.

In ending this volume, I place the burden back upon those who assert Philemon's authenticity. We have seen that claims of the letter being manifestly "Pauline" in style, structure, and contents are largely flawed and can conceivably be read (better read, I would argue) on the hypothesis of inauthenticity. The claim of difficulty when imagining reasons to fabricate Philemon better showcases either various scholars' unwillingness to imagine alternative scenarios, or a lack of imagination in considering what forgers might create and why. Indeed, we have seen multiple potential reasons why a clever forger might have fabricated this letter. Given this, I am curious to see what convincing pro-Philemon arguments could be offered. A mere rebuttal, as noted above, is not enough to crown authenticity correct. If one cannot show convincing pro arguments for Philemon's authenticity, then we are no more justified in considering it authentic than we are inauthentic. In short, we may very well have to concede that this tiny letter, filled with endless mystery, may even be enigmatic in its origins.

5. E.g., Knox, "Philemon and the Authenticity of Colossians"; Johnson, *Constructing Paul.*

6. Walker, *Interpolations in the Pauline Letters,* 57–58.

And that, ultimately, is the purpose of this volume. I do not expect to change a consensus on the authenticity of Philemon; I merely wish for academics to cease taking authenticity for granted, to justify and ground their positions rather than wishing them into reality based on nearly nothing. Authenticity is not a valid assumption—it must be grounded and argued for, and if one cannot do that, one has no reason to take something as authentic in the first place. Dismissing the issue of authenticity in a single sentence, as some commentators have done, or assuming it without comment at all characterizes authenticity as dogma more than as a legitimate scholarly argument. The foundations of a consensus must be sturdier than sand if it is to stay upright.

Appendix

Translation of Philemon

I wish to present here my best attempt at a translation of Philemon, which I refer to throughout this book. Included are some explanatory notes based on the Nestle-Aland *Novum Testamentum Graece* (twenty-eighth edition), which I refer readers back to for additional clarification. I have bracketed passages and terms that Holtzmann, Hausrath, Brückner, and Waugh proposed as being interpolations,[1] and I have also rendered a version of the letter that omits the conjectured glosses. This, I think, provides a rather interesting alternative reading of the letter.

TRANSLATION OF THE EPISTLE TO PHILEMON

(1) Paul, [a prisoner[2] of Jesus Christ, and brother Timothy]

To our beloved and coworker Philemon [(2) and to our sister Apphia,[3] and to our fellow soldier Archippus, and to the assembly[4] at your house.]

---

1. Holtzmann, "Brief an den Philemon"; Hausrath, *History of New Testament Times*, 122–23; Brückner, *Chronologische Reihenfolge*, 200–203; Waugh, "Philemon."

2. Often altered to "apostle" and "slave" in other manuscripts (in some cases, combinations).

3. Sometimes the word "beloved" appears prior to Apphia.

4. I chose to translate this as "assembly" rather than "church" to avoid the modern connotation of a church building. This was, for all intents and purposes, meant as an assembly of individuals in a personal home.

(3) Grace and peace be on you all[5] from our father God and lord Jesus Christ. [(4) I thank my God when I remember you in my prayers, (5) as I hear of your love and faith that you have toward the lord Jesus and toward all of the dedicated[6] (6) so your fellowship of faith might be effective in knowing every good that we have in Christ.] (7) I have great joy and encouragement due to your love, because the hearts of the dedicated have been refreshed by you, brother.

(8) Thus, (though I am)[7] bold enough in Christ to order you to do what is befitting, (9) yet I would rather appeal (to you)[8] for love's sake, [I Paul being old and now a prisoner of Jesus Christ] (10) appeal to you for Onesimus, my child I begot [while in chains,] (11) who was useless to you, but now has utility to me and you,[9] [(12) (and)[10] whom I am returning to you in person.[11]]

(13) I wished to keep him myself so that he might serve me [while in the chains of the gospel] on your behalf. (14) However, I did not wish to do so without your consent, lest any good you do be according to force rather than willingness. (15) Perhaps because of this he was separated from

5. "You all" is my rendering of the plural second-person personal pronoun. Because English has no singular second-person pronoun ("you" is a defective plural pronoun functioning in both capacities), I wished to remove ambiguity with the insertion of "all," which more explicitly denotes the multitude of individuals referred to in the original passage.

6. Typically, the ending word is translated as "saints," but I have rendered it "dedicated." Because the original term is an adjective, I avoided the misleading noun of "saints." Note, modern translations like the NIV actually modify this in translation, as the passage implies having faith specifically in the sainted Christ-followers (likely also referring to previous prophets). For example, the NIV renders Philemon 5 as "because I hear about your love for all his holy people and your faith in the Lord Jesus." Here, the Christ-followers of Philemon's household have faith both in Jesus and the saints; this partition is not accurate to the original Greek.

7. Paul does not directly refer to himself here, but it is necessary context for the sentence to cohere when translated.

8. Not in the original Greek.

9. Here the utility also very likely comes with a sexual component, where Paul is expressing that Onesimus will be sexually submissive as a slave. Marchal's examination ("Usefulness of an Onesimus") indicates that the usage of εὔχρηστος carried a double entendre in such situations. We should not ignore this specific component, as it was endemic to the institution of slavery in antiquity.

10. The conjunction is not present in the Greek.

11. This seemingly refers to Onesimus' person. However, if Hausrath is correct that all mentions of Paul's imprisonment are interpolations, this could instead refer to Paul bringing Onesimus back himself after having sent this letter ahead.

you for a time so that you might have him eternally, (16) no longer as a slave but greater than a slave, a beloved brother. He is very precious [to me especially], however how much more to you, both in the flesh and in the Lord. (17) If, thus, you think me a partner, receive him as (you would)[12] me.

(18) If, however, he has wronged you or owes you, charge this to me.[13] (19) [I, Paul, write this with my own hand.] I shall repay it, that I not say that you owe yourself to me also.[14] (20) Yea, brother let me profit from you in the Lord (and) refresh my heart in Christ! [(21) Sure of your obedience, I write you, knowing you will do more than what I say you will.[15]]

[(22) Additionally, prepare a room for me, as I hope that through prayer I will be returned to you all.]

[(23) Epaphras, [my fellow prisoner in Christ Jesus,] sends greetings to you, (24) (as do)[16] my fellow workers Mark, Aristarchus, Demas, (and)[17] Luke.]

(25) The grace of the Lord Jesus Christ be with your spirit, Amen.

WITHOUT PROPOSED HOLTZMANN/HAUSRATH/ BRÜCKNER/WAUGH INTERPOLATIONS

(1) Paul,

To our beloved and coworker Philemon

(3) Grace and peace be on you all from our father God and lord Jesus Christ. (7) I have great joy and encouragement due to your love, because the hearts of the dedicated have been refreshed by you, brother.

(8) Thus, (though I am) bold enough in Christ to order you to do what is befitting, (9) yet I would rather appeal (to you) for love's sake. (10) I

12. Not in the original Greek. Added for clarification.

13. Here the implication seems to be that some damage or harm prevented Onesimus from simply returning to reconcile their relationship. Being an ancient letter on slavery, blame is automatically put on the slave, not the owner.

14. On my reading, "Paul" is probably implying that he converted Philemon, and due to this there is an implied debt. "Paul" is bringing these debts into parallel, as in both cases he is taking on the debts of someone else.

15. This refers to the above directions "Paul" gives him. Here the implication is that the slave owner is to go beyond these basic rules of reconciliation.

16. Not present in the Greek, but added for clarity.

17. The conjunction is not present in the Greek—added for the sake of clarity in English grammar.

appeal to you for Onesimus, my child I begot (11) who was useless to you, but now has utility to me and you.

(13) I wished to keep him myself so that he might serve me on your behalf. (14) However, I did not wish to do so without your consent, lest any good you do be according to force rather than willingness. (15) Perhaps because of this he was separated from you for a time so that you might have him eternally, (16) no longer as a slave but greater than a slave, a beloved brother. He is very precious, however how much more to you, both in the flesh and in the Lord. (17) If, thus, you think me a partner, receive him as (you would) me.

(18) If, however, he has wronged you or owes you, charge this to me. (19) I shall repay it, that I not say that you owe yourself to me also. (20) Yea, brother let me profit from you in the Lord (and) refresh my heart in Christ! (25) The grace of the Lord Jesus Christ be with your spirit, Amen.

Bibliography

Alford, Henry. *The Greek Testament: With a Critically Revised Text*. 4 vols. 3rd ed. London: n.p., 1862.

Atwill, Joseph. *Shakespeare's Secret Messiah*. Self-published, 2014.

Aune, David E. "The Problem of Equality in the Church and Society." In *From Judaism to Christianity: Tradition and Transition*, edited by Patricia Walters, 153–84. Leiden: Brill, 2011.

Baird, William. *History of New Testament Research*, vol. 1, *From Deism to Tübingen*. Minneapolis: Fortress, 1992.

Balabanski, Vicky. "Where Is Philemon? The Case for a Logical Fallacy in the Correlation of the Data in Philemon and Colossians 1.1–2; 4.7–18." *Journal for the Study of the New Testament* 38.2 (2015) 131–50.

Barclay, John M. G. *Colossians and Philemon*. London: T. & T. Clark, 2004.

Bartchy, S. Scott. "Philemon, Epistle to." In *The Anchor Bible Dictionary*, edited by David Noel Freedman, 5:305–10. New York: Doubleday, 1992.

Barth, Markus, and Helmut Blanke. *The Letter to Philemon*. Eerdmans Critical Commentary. Grand Rapids: Eerdmans, 2000.

Bate, H. N. "Chronicle." *Journal of Theological Studies* 4 (1903) 301–9.

Bauer, Bruno. *Christ and the Caesars*. Translated by Frank E. Schacht. Charleston, SC: Alexander Davidonis, 1998.

———. *Kritik der paulinischen Briefe*. 3 vols. Berlin: Hempel, 1850–52.

Baur, F. C. *Paul, the Apostle of Jesus Christ*. Translated by Robert F. Brown and Peter C. Hodgson. Eugene, OR: Cascade, 2021.

Beale, G. K. *Colossians and Philemon*. Baker Exegetical Commentary on the New Testament. Grand Rapids: Baker, 2019.

Beavis, Mary Ann. *The First Christian Slave: Onesimus in Context*. Eugene, OR: Cascade, 2021.

BeDuhn, Jason D. *The First New Testament: Marcion's Scriptural Canon*. Salem, OR: Polebridge, 2013.

Bell, Brigidda. "The Cost of Baptism? The Case for Paul's Ritual Compensation." *Journal for the Study of the New Testament* 42.4 (2020) 431–52.

Bennett, DeRobigne Mortimer. *The Gods and Religions of Ancient and Modern Times*. 2 vols. New York: D. M. Bennett, 1880.

Bernier, Jonathan. *Rethinking the Dates of the New Testament: The Evidence for Early Composition*. Grand Rapids: Baker, 2022.

Bibliography

———. "When Paul Met Sergius: An Assessment of Douglas Campbell's Pauline Chronology for the Years 36 to 37." *Journal of Biblical Literature* 138.4 (2019) 829–43.

Bianchini, Francesco. "The Crux Interpretum of 1 Cor 15:29: What Is at Stake and a Proposal." *Verbum Vitae* 40.4 (2022) 1007–16.

Bilby, Mark G. "Pliny's Correspondence and the Acts of the Apostles: An Intertextual Relationship?" In *Luke on Jesus, Paul and Christianity: What Did He Really Know?* edited by Joseph Verheyden and John S. Kloppenborg, 147–70. Leuven: Peeters, 2017.

Bird, Michael F. *Colossians & Philemon: A New Covenant Commentary.* Cambridge: Lutterworth, 2009.

Boer, Roland, and Christina Petterson. "Hand of the Master: Of Slaveholders and the Slave-Relation." In *Class Struggle in the New Testament,* edited by Robert J. Myles, 139–52. Lanham: Lexington, 2019.

———. *Time of Troubles: A New Economic Framework for Early Christianity.* Minneapolis: Fortress, 2017.

Bolland, Gerardus Johannes Petrus Josephus. *De evangelische Jozua: Eene poging tot aanwijzing van den oorsprong des Christendoms.* Leiden: A. H. Adriani, 1907.

Boring, M. Eugene. *An Introduction to the New Testament: History, Literature, Theology.* Louisville: Westminster John Knox, 2012.

Bray, Gerald L., trans. *Commentaries on Galatians–Philemon, Ambrosiaster.* Downers Grove, IL: InterVarsity, 2009.

Britt, Matthew, and Jaaron Wingo. *Christ before Jesus: Evidence for the Second-Century Origins of Christianity.* N.p.: Cooper & Samuels, 2024.

Brodie, Thomas L. *Beyond the Quest for the Historical Jesus: Memoir of a Discovery.* Sheffield: Sheffield Phoenix, 2012.

———. *The Birthing of the New Testament: The Intertextual Development of the New Testament Writings.* Sheffield: Sheffield Phoenix, 2004.

Brodie, Thomas L., Dennis R. MacDonald, and Stanley E. Porter, eds. *The Intertextuality of the Epistles: Explorations of Theory and Practice.* Sheffield: Sheffield Phoenix, 2006.

Brogdon, Lewis. *A Companion to Philemon.* Eugene, OR: Cascade, 2018.

Brookins, Timothy A. *Ancient Rhetoric and the Style of Paul's Letters: A Reference Book.* Eugene, OR: Cascade, 2022.

Brown, William Montgomery. *Communism and Christianism: Analyzed and Contrasted from the Marxian and Darwinian Points of View.* Galion: Bradford-Brown Educational Company, n.d.

Bruce, F. F. *Paul: Apostle of the Heart Set Free.* Carlisle: Paternoster, 1977.

Brückner, Wilhelm. *Die chronologische Reihenfolge, in welcher die Briefe des Neuen Testaments verfasst sind.* Haarlem: F. Bohn, 1890.

———. *The Epistles to the Colossians, to Philemon, and to the Ephesians.* NICNT. Grand Rapids: Eerdmans, 1984.

Byron, John. "The Letter to Philemon: Paul's Strategy for Forging the Ties of Kinship." In *Jesus and Paul: Global Perspectives in Honor of James D. G. Dunn for His 70th Birthday,* 205–16. London: T. & T. Clark, 2009.

Callahan, Allan Dwight. *Embassay of Onesimus: The Letter of Paul to Philemon.* Valley Forge, PA: Trinity, 1997.

Campbell, Douglas A. *Framing Paul: An Epistolary Biography.* Grand Rapids: Eerdmans, 2014.

Bibliography

Carrier, Richard. *On the Historicity of Jesus: Why We Might Have Reason for Doubt.* Sheffield: Sheffield Phoenix, 2014.

Carter, John W. *The Pastoral Epistles 1, 2 Timothy, Titus, & Philemon: Principles of Biblical Servant Leadership.* Disciple's Bible Commentary. Hayesville, NC: American Journal of Biblical Theology, 2022.

Corke-Webster, James. "The Early Reception of Pliny the Younger in Tertullian of Carthage and Eusebius of Caesarea." *The Classical Quarterly* 67.1 (2017) 247–62.

Costa, C. D. N., ed. *Greek Fictional Letters: A Selection with Introduction, Translation and Commentary.* Oxford: Oxford University Press, 2001.

Cousar, Charles B. *Philippians and Philemon: A Commentary.* New Testament Library. Louisville: Westminster John Knox, 2009.

Crossley, James G. *Why Christianity Happened: A Sociohistorical Account of Christian Origins (26–50 CE).* Louisville: Westminster John Knox, 2006.

Crüsemann, Marlene. *The Pseudepigraphical Letters to the Thessalonians.* Translated by Linda M. Maloney. London: T. & T. Clark, 2010.

Cutner, Herbert. *Jesus: God, Man or Myth?* Escondido, CA: Book Tree, 2000.

Davis, Henry. *Creating Christianity: A Weapon of Ancient Rome.* Self-published, 2020.

Davis, Kipp. "Caves of Dispute: Patterns of Correspondence and Suspicion in the Post-2002 'Dead Sea Scrolls' Fragments." *Dead Sea Discoveries* 24.2 (2017) 229–70.

Decock, Paul B. "The Reception of the Letter to Philemon in the Early Church: Origen, Jerome, Chrysostom and Augustine." In *Philemon in Perspective: Interpreting a Pauline Letter*, edited by D. Francois Tolmie, 273–88. Berlin: Walter de Gruyter, 2010.

Detering, Hermann. "The Dutch Radical Approach to the Pauline Epistles." *Journal of Higher Criticism* 3.2 (1996) 163–93.

———. *The Fabricated Paul: Early Christianity in the Twilight.* Translated by Darrell J. Doughty. Independently published, 2018.

———. *Inszenierte Fälschungen: Die Paulusbriefe in der holländischen Radikalkritik.* Independently Published, 2018.

———. *Paulusbriefe ohne Paulus? Die Paulusbriefe in der holländischen Radikalkritik.* Frankfurt am Main: Peter Lang, 1992.

Dorion, Louis-André. "The Rise and Fall of the Socratic Problem." In *The Cambridge Companion to Socrates*, edited by Donald R. Morrison, 1–23. Cambridge: Cambridge University Press, 2011.

Doughty, Darrell J. "Pauline Paradigms and Pauline Authenticity." *Journal of Higher Criticism* 1 (1994) 95–128.

Downs, David J. "Justification, Good Works, and Creation in Clement of Rome's Appropriation of Romans 5–6." *New Testament Studies* 59 (2013) 415–32.

Drews, Arthur. *The Christ Myth.* Translated by C. Delisle Burns. 3rd ed. London: T. Fisher Unwin, 1910.

———. *The Witnesses to the Historicity of Jesus.* Translated by Joseph McCabe. London: Watts, 1912.

Dunn, James D. G. *The Epistles to the Colossians and to Philemon: A Commentary on the Greek Text.* NIGTC. Grand Rapids: Eerdmans, 1996.

Ebner, Martin. *Der Brief an Philemon.* Evangelisch-Katholische Kommentar zum Neuen Testament. Göttingen: Vandenhoeck & Ruprecht, 2017.

Ehorn, Seth M. *Philemon.* Evangelical Exegetical Commentary. Digital ed. Bellingham, WA: Lexham, 2011.

Ehrman, Bart D. *Forgery and Counterforgery: The Use of Literary Deceit in Early Christian Polemics*. Oxford: Oxford University Press, 2013.

Elmer, Ian J. "I, Tertius: Secretary or Co-Author of Romans." *Australian Biblical Review* 56 (2008) 45–60.

Engels, Friedrich. "On the History of Early Christianity." In *On Religion*, by Karl Marx and Friedrich Engels, 316–47. Mineola: Dover, 2008.

Epictetus. *Discourses Books 1–2*. Translated by W. A. Oldfather. LCL 131. Cambridge, MA: Harvard University Press, 1998.

Erdman, Charles R. *The Epistles of Paul to the Colossians and to Philemon*. Erdman Commentaries on the New Testament. Grand Rapids: Baker, 1966.

Eurell, John-Christian. "The Second Imprisonment of Paul: Fiction or Reality?" *Scottish Journal of Theology* 76 (2023) 230–39.

Evans, Elizabeth E. *The Christ Myth: A Study*. New York: Truth Seeker, 1900.

Evanson, Edward. *The Dissonance of the Four Generally Received Evangelists and the Evidence of Their Respective Authenticity, Examined*. Gloucester: D. Walker, 1805.

———. *A Letter to the Right Reverend the Lord Bishop of Litchfield and Coventry*. London: B. Law, 1777.

Ewald, Paul. *Die Briefe des Paulus an die Epheser, Kolosser, und Philemon*. Kommentar zum Neuen Testament. Leipzig: A. Deichert'sche Verlagsbuchhandlung Nachf., 1910.

Fee, Gordon. *Pauline Christology: An Exegetical-Theological Study*. Peabody, MA: Hendrickson, 2007.

Fitzmyer, Joseph. *The Acts of the Apostles*. New York: Doubleday, 1998.

———. *The Letter to Philemon: A New Translation with Introduction and Commentary*. Anchor Bible. New York: Doubleday, 2000.

Fortenbaugh, William W. *Aristotle's Practical Side: On His Psychology, Ethics, Politics and Rhetoric*. Leiden: Brill, 2006.

Gallagher, Edmon L., and John D. Meade. *The Biblical Canon Lists from Early Christianity: Text and Analysis*. Oxford: Oxford University Press, 2017.

Garland, David E. *Colossians and Philemon*. NIV Application Commentary. Grand Rapids: Zondervan, 1998.

Glancy, Jennifer A. *Slavery as Moral Problem: In the Early Church and Today*. Minneapolis: Fortress, 2011.

———. *Slavery in Early Christianity*. Minneapolis: Fortress, 2006.

———. *Slavery in Early Christianity*. Expanded ed. Minneapolis: Fortress, 2024.

Gnilka, Joachim. *Der Philemonbrief*. Freiburg: Herder, 1982.

Goguel, Maurice. *Jesus the Nazarene: Myth or History?* Translated by Frederick Stephens. Amherst, MA: Prometheus, 2006.

Goodacre, Mark. "Fatigue in the Synoptics." *New Testament Studies* 44.1 (1998) 45–58.

Gorday, Peter, ed. *Colossians, 1–2 Thessalonians, 1–2 Timothy, Titus, Philemon*. Ancient Christian Commentary on Scripture. Downers Grove, IL: InterVarsity, 2000.

Green, Colin A. "Paul's Letter to Philemon: Manumission . . . or What?" *Journal of Greco-Roman Christianity and Judaism* 18 (2022) 92–112.

Greer, Rowan A., trans. *Commentary on the Minor Pauline Epistles, Theodore of Mopsuestia*. Atlanta: Society of Biblical Literature, 2010.

Hagar, Harry James. "The Radical School of Dutch New Testament Criticism." PhD dissertation. University of Chicago, 1933.

Hahn, Scott, and Curtis Mitch. *The Ignatius Catholic Study Bible*. 2nd Catholic ed. San Francisco: Ignatius, 2010.

Bibliography

Hamm, Dennis. *Philippians, Colossians, Philemon*. Catholic Commentary on Sacred Scripture. Grand Rapids: Baker, 2013.

Hansen, C. M. "The Authenticity of Philemon: The Problems and Assumptions in the Consensus Position." *Revista Bíblica* (forthcoming).

————. "From Rags to Reverend: The Life of Jens Peter Hansen (1871–1903)." *American Journal of Biblical Theology* 23 (38) (2022). Digital ed.

————. "The Number of the Myth: A Defence of the Ahistoricity of the Neronian Persecution." *Journal of Early Christian History* 13.2 (2023) 1–21.

————. "Popular History and Roman Provenance: A Discussion of the Works of Atwill, Piso, Gallus, and Davis." *Alternative Spirituality & Religion Review* (forthcoming).

————. "The Problem of Annals 15.44: On the Plinian Origin of Tacitus's Information on Christians." *Journal of Early Christian History* 13.1 (2023) 62–80.

Harding, Mark. "Disputed and Undisputed Letters of Paul." In *The Pauline Canon*, edited by Stanley E. Porter, 129–68. Leiden: Brill, 2004.

Hart, Patrick. *A Prolegomenon to the Study of Paul*. Leiden: Brill, 2020.

Hausrath, Adolf. *A History of the New Testament Times*. Vol. 4. Translated by L. Huxley. London: Williams and Norgate, 1895.

Head, Peter M. "Onesimus the Letter Carrier and the Initial Reception of Paul's Letter to Philemon." *Journal of Theological Studies* 71.2 (2020) 628–56.

Heine, Ronald E. "In Search of Origen's Commentary on Philemon." *Harvard Theological Review* 93.2 (2000) 117–33.

Herron, Thomas J. *Clement and the Early Church of Rome: On the Dating of Clement's First Epistle to the Corinthians*. Originally published 1988. Steubenville, OH: Emmaus Road, 2018.

Hill, Robert Charles, trans. *Theodoret of Cyrus: Commentary on the Letters of St. Paul*. Vol. 2. Brookline: Holy Cross Orthodox, 2001.

Hoehner, Harold W. "Did Paul Write Galatians?" In *History and Exegesis: New Testament Essays in Honor of Dr. E. Earle Ellis for His 80th Birthday*, edited by Sang-Won Son, 150–69. London: T. & T. Clark, 2006.

Holtzmann, Heinrich J. "Der Brief an den Philemon." *Zeitschrift für wissenschaftliche Theologie* 16 (1873) 428–41.

————. "Introduction to the Epistle to Philemon." In *A Short Protestant Commentary on the Books of the New Testament: With General and Special Introductions*, edited by Paul Wilhelm Schmidt and Franz von Holzendorff, translated by Francis Henry Jones, 3:111–14. London: Williams and Norgate, 1884.

Immendörfer, Michael. *Ephesians and Artemis: The Cult of the Great Goddess of Ephesus as the Epistle's Context*. Tübingen: Mohr Siebeck, 2017.

Ip, Alex Hon Ho. *A Socio-Rhetorical Interpretation of the Letter to Philemon in Light of New Institutional Economics*. Tübingen: Mohr Siebeck, 2017.

Johnson, Edwin P. *Antiqua Mater: A Study of Christian Origins*. London: Trübner, 1887.

————. *The Pauline Epistles: Re-Studied and Explained*. London: Watts, 1896.

Johnson, Luke Timothy. *Constructing Paul*. Vol. 1. Grand Rapids: Eerdmans, 2020.

Julian. "The Popular Religious Faith." *The Agnostic* 1.1 (1885) 28–32.

Kalthoff, Albert. *The Rise of Christianity*. Translated by Joseph McCabe. London: Watts, 1907.

Kautsky, Karl. *Foundations of Christianity*. Translated by Henry F. Mins. New York: Russell & Russell, 1953.

Keegan, Terence J. *First and Second Timothy, Titus, Philemon*. New Collegeville Bible Commentary. Collegeville, MN: Liturgical, 2005.

Kenny, Anthony. *A Stylometric Study of the New Testament*. Oxford: Clarendon, 1984.

Killen, William P. "The Ignatian Letters Entirely Spurious." *Journal of Higher Criticism* 8.1 (2001) 144–58.

Knapp, Robert. *Invisible Romans*. Cambridge, MA: Harvard University Press, 2011.

Knopf, Rudolf. *Commentary on the Didache and 1–2 Clement*. Translated by Jacob N. Cerone. Eugene, OR: Pickwick, 2023.

Knox, John. *Philemon Among the Letters of Paul*. London: Collins, 1960.

———. "Philemon and the Authenticity of Colossians." *Journal of Religion* 18.2 (1938) 144–60.

Kok, Michael J. *The Beloved Apostle? The Transformation of the Apostle John into the Fourth Evangelist*. Eugene, OR: Cascade, 2017.

———. "Justin Martyr and the Authorship of Luke's Gospel." *Journal of Greco-Roman Christianity and Judaism* 18 (2022) 9–36.

Köstenberger, Andreas, J. L. Scott Kellum, and Charles L Quarles. *The Cradle, the Cross, and the Crown*. Nashville: B&H, 2009.

Kreinecker, Christina M. "The Imitation Hypothesis: Pseudepigraphic Remarks on 2 Thessalonians with Help from Documentary Papyri." In *Paul and Pseudepigraphy*, edited by Stanley E. Porter and Gregory P. Fewster, 197–219. Leiden: Brill, 2013.

Kreitzer, Larry J. *Philemon*. Readings: A New Biblical Commentary. Sheffield: Sheffield Phoenix, 2008.

Kroonenberg, Pieter M. *Multivariate Humanities*. Cham: Springer, 2021.

Kryvelev, Iosif A. *Christ: Myth or Reality?* Translated by S. Kotlobye. Moscow: USSR Academy of Sciences, 1987.

Laird, Benjamin P. *The Pauline Corpus in Early Christianity: Its Formation, Publication, and Circulation*. Peabody, MA: Hendrickson, 2022.

Laken, Katarina. "An Authorship Study on the Letters of Saint Paul." Thesis. Radboud University, 2018.

Lemaire, Samuel. *Etude sur l'épître de S. Paul à Philémon*. Lausanne: Imprimerie Georges Bridel, 1869.

Lenzman, *L'Origine du christianisme*. Translated by L. Piatigorski. Moscow: Editions en languages etrangeres, 1961.

Leppä, Outi. *The Making of Colossians: A Study on the Formation and Purpose of a Deutero-Pauline Letter*. Göttingen: Vandenhoeck & Ruprecht, 2005.

Letteney, Mark. "Authenticity and Authority: The Case for Dismantling a Dubious Correlation." In *Rethinking 'Authority' in Late Antiquity: Authorship, Law, and Transmission in Jewish and Christian Tradition*, edited by A. J. Berkovitz and Mark Letteney, 33–56. New York: Routledge, 2018.

Lingelbach, John F. *The Date of the Muratorian Fragment: An Inference to the Best Explanation*. Denver: Global Center for Religious Research, 2020.

Litton, Edward Arthur. "Philemon, Epistle to." In *The Imperial Bible Dictionary*, edited by Patrick Fairbairn, 2:604. London: Blackie, 1866.

Lohse, Eduard. *Colossians and Philemon*. Translated by William R. Poehlmann and Robert J. Karris. Hermeneia. Philadelphia: Fortress, 1971.

Loman, Abraham Dirk. "Quaestiones Paulinae: Prolegomena. Noodzakelijkheid eener herziening van de grondslagen onzer kennis van het oor spronkelijk Paulinisme." *Theologisch Tijdschrift* 16 (1882) 141–85.

Bibliography

————. "Quaestiones Paulinae: Onderzoek naar de echtheid van den Brief ann de Galatiërs, 1ste hoofdstuk. De uitwendige bewijsmiddelen." *Theologisch Tijdschrift* 16 (1882) 302–28, 452–87.

————. "Quaestiones Paulinae: Tweede vervolg en slot van het eerste hoofdstuk." *Theologisch Tijdschrift* 17 (1883) 14–57.

————. "Quaestiones Paulinae II, P. 1: Terugblik en overgang tot het tweede hoofdstuk." *Theologisch Tijdschrift* 20 (1886) 42–113.

Lookadoo, Jonathon. "The Date and Authenticity of the Ignatian Letters: An Outline of Recent Discussions." *Currents in Biblical Research* 19.1 (2020) 88–114.

————. "Polycarp, Paul, and the Letters to Timothy." *Novum Testamentum* 59.4 (2017) 366–83.

MacDonald, Margaret Y. "Kinship and Family in the New Testament World." In *Understanding the Social World of the New Testament*, edited by Dietmar Neufeld and Richard E. DeMaris, 29–43. New York: Routledge, 2010.

Marchal, Joseph A. "Slaves as Wo/men and Unmen: Reflecting Upon Euodia, Syntiche, and Epaphroditus in Philippi." In *The People Beside Paul: The Philippian Assembly and History from Below*, edited by Joseph A. Marchal, 141–76. Atlanta: SBL, 2015.

————. "The Usefulness of an Onesimus: The Sexual Use of Slaves and Paul's Letter to Philemon." *Journal of Biblical Literature* 130.4 (2011) 749–70.

Martens, John W. "Ignatius and Onesimus: John Knox Reconsidered." *Second Century* 9 (1992) 73–86.

Mastnjak, Nathan. *Before the Scrolls: A Material Approach to Israel's Prophetic Library.* Oxford: Oxford University Press, 2023.

McDonald, H. Dermot. *Commentary on Colossians & Philemon.* Waco, TX: Word, 1980.

McDowell, Sean. *The Fate of the Apostles: Examining the Martyrdom Accounts of the Closest Followers of Jesus.* Farham: Ashgate, 2015.

McGuire, Frank R. "Did Paul Write Galatians?" *Hibbert Journal* 66 (1967–68) 52–57.

McKnight, Scot. *The Letter to Philemon.* New International Commentary on the New Testament. Grand Rapids: Eerdmans, 2017.

Mealand, D. L., "The Extent of the Pauline Corpus: A Multivariate Approach." *Journal for the Study of the New Testament* 59 (1995) 61–92.

Melick, Richard R. *Philippians, Colossians, Philemon.* New American Commentary. Nashville: B&H, 1991.

Migliore, Daniel L. *Philippians and Philemon.* Belief: A Theological Commentary of the Bible. Louisville: Westminster John Knox, 2014.

Mitchell, Matthew W. "In the Footsteps of Paul: Scriptural and Apostolic Authority in Ignatius of Antioch." *Journal of Early Christian Studies* 14.1 (2006) 27–45.

Moo, Douglas J. *The Letters to the Colossians and to Philemon.* Pillar New Testament Commentary. Grand Rapids: Eerdmans, 2008.

Moss, Candida. *God's Ghostwriters: Enslaved Christians and the Making of the Bible.* New York: Little, Brown, 2024.

————. *The Myth of Persecution: How Early Christians Invented a Story of Martyrdom.* New York: HarperOne, 2013.

————. "On the Dating of Polycarp: Rethinking the Place of the Martyrdom of Polycarp in the History of Christianity." *Early Christianity* 1 (2010) 539–74.

————. "The Secretary: Enslaved Workers, Stenography, and the Production of Early Christian Literature." *Journal of Theological Studies* 74.1 (2023) 20–56.

Bibliography

Moule, H. C. G. *The Epistles to the Colossians and to Philemon: With Introduction and Notes.* Cambridge: Cambridge University Press, 1893.

Müller, Jacobus Johannes. *The Epistles of Paul to the Philippians and to Philemon: The English Text with Introduction, Exposition and Notes.* Grand Rapids: Eerdmans, 1955.

Müller, Peter. *Der Brief an Philemon.* Kritisch-exegetischer Kommentar uber das Neue Testament. Göttingen: Vandenhoeck & Ruprecht, 2011.

Neumann, Kenneth J. *The Authenticity of the Pauline Epistles in the Light of Stylostatistical Analysis.* Atlanta: Scholars, 1990.

Neutel, Karin B., and Peter-Ben Smit. "Paul, Imprisonment and Crisis: Crisis and its Negotiation as a Lens for Reading Philippians." *Journal for the Study of the New Testament* 44.1 (2021) 31–55.

Nongbri, Brent. *God's Library: The Archaeology of the Earliest Christian Manuscripts.* New Haven, CT: Yale University Press, 2018.

O'Brien, Peter T. *Colossians, Philemon.* Word Biblical Commentary. Waco, TX: Word, 1982.

Økland, Jorunn. "Textual Reproduction as Surplus Value: Paul on Pleasing Christ and Spouses, in Light of Simon de Beauvoir." In *Marxist Feminist Criticism of the Bible*, edited by Roland Boer and Jorunn Økland, 182–203. Sheffield: Sheffield Phoenix, 2008.

O'Neill, J. C. "Paul Wrote Some of All, but Not All of Any." In *The Pauline Canon*, edited by Stanley E. Porter, 169–88. Leiden: Brill, 2004.

———. *Paul's Letter to the Romans.* New York: Penguin, 1975.

———. *The Recovery of Paul's Letter to the Galatians.* London: SPCK, 1972.

Osiek, Carolyn. *Philippians and Philemon.* Abingdon New Testament Commentaries. Nashville: Abingdon, 2000.

Paine, Thomas. *The Works of Thomas Paine.* Philadelphia: James Carey, 1797.

Paley, Justin. "Questioning the Pauline Authorship of Philemon: Crackpot Theory or Plausible Alternative?" *Expository Times* 134.1 (2022) 11–20.

Pao, David W. *Colossians & Philemon.* Exegetical Commentary on the New Testament. Grand Rapids: Zondervan Academic, 2012.

Patzia, Arthur G. *Ephesians, Colossians, Philemon.* Understanding the Bible Commentary Series. Grand Rapids: Baker, 2011.

Peabody, David Barrett. "H.J. Holtzmann and his European Colleagues: Aspects of Nineteenth-Century European Discussion of Gospel Origins." In *Biblical Studies and the Shifting of Paradigms, 1850–1914*, edited by Henning Graf Raventlow and William Farmer, 50–131. Sheffield: Sheffield Academic, 1995.

Pfleiderer, Otto. *Der Paulinismus: Ein Beitrag zur Geschichte der urchristlichen Theologie.* Leipzig: Fues's, 1873.

———. *Primitive Christianity: Its Historical Writings and Teachings in Their Historical Connections.* Trans. W. Montgomery and W. D. Morrison. 4 Vols; Clifton: Reference, 1965.

———. *Der Urchristentum, seine Schriften und Lehren, in geschichtlichem Zusammenhang.* Berlin: Georg Reimer, 1887.

Pierson, Allard, and Samuel Naber. *Verisimilia: Lacerum conditionem Novi Testamenti exemplis illustrarunt et ab origine repetierunt.* Amsterdam: Van Kampen, 1886.

Piso, Roman, and Jay Gallus. *Piso Christ: A Book of the New Classical Scholarship.* Victoria, BC: Trafford, 2010.

Bibliography

Price, Robert M. *The Amazing Colossal Apostle: The Search for the Historical Paul.* Salt Lake City: Signature, 2012.

—————. *Bart Ehrman Interpreted: How One Radical New Testament Scholar Understands Another.* Durham, NC: Pitchstone, 2018.

—————. "Does the Christ Myth Theory Require and Early Date for the Pauline Epistles?" In *'Is This Not the Carpenter?' The Question of the Historicity of the Figure of Jesus,* edited by Thomas L. Thompson and Thomas S. Verenna, 95–116. Sheffield: Equinox, 2011.

—————. *Holy Fable,* vol. 3, *The Epistles and the Apocalypse Undistorted by Faith.* N.p.: Mindvendor, 2018.

—————. *The Pre-Nicene New Testament: Fifty-Four Formative Texts.* Salt Lake City: Signature, 2006.

Priestley, Joseph. *The Theological and Miscellaneous Works of Joseph Priestley.* Edited by John Towill Rutt. Vol. 20. Hackney: G. Smallfield, 1831.

Rasimus, Tuomas, Troels Engberg-Pedersen, Ismo Dunderberg, eds. *Stoicism in Early Christianity.* Grand Rapids: Baker, 2010.

Remsburg, John E. *The Bible.* New York: Truth Seeker, 1907.

Reuter, Rainer. *Synopse zu den Briefen des Neuen Testaments.* Frankfurt am Main: Peter Lang, 1997.

Robertson, Archibald. *The Bible and its Background.* 2 vols. 2nd ed. London: Watts, 1949.

Rosenmeyer, Patricia A. *Ancient Greek Literary Letters: Selections in Translation.* New York: Routledge, 2006.

Rothschild, Clare K. *The Muratorian Fragment: Text, Translation, Commentary.* Tübingen: Mohr Siebeck, 2022.

Roy, Ashley, and Paul Robertson. "Applying Cosine Similarity to Paul's Letters: Mathematically Modelling Formal and Stylistic Similarities." In *New Approaches to Textual and Image Analysis in Early Jewish and Christian Studies,* edited by Sara Schulthess, Garrick V. Allen, Paul Dilley, and Peter M. Phillips, 88–117. Leiden: Brill, 2023.

Rylands, L. Gordon. *A Critical Analysis of the Four Chief Pauline Epistles: Romans, First and Second Corinthians and Galatians.* London: Watts, 1929.

Salm, René. *NazarethGate: Quack Archaeology, Holy Hoaxes, and the Invented Town of Jesus.* Cranford, NJ: American Atheist, 2015.

Savoy, Jacques. "Authorship of Pauline Epistles Revisited." *Journal of the Association for Information Science and Technology* 70.10 (2019) 1089–97.

Schaff, Philip, ed. *A Select Library of the Nicene and Post-Nicene Fathers of the Christian Church.* Grand Rapids: Eerdmans, 1956.

Scheck, Thomas P., trans. *St. Jerome's Commentaries on Galatians, Titus, and Philemon.* Notre Dame, IN: University of Notre Dame Press, 2010.

Scheidel, Walter. "Real Slave Prices and the Relative Cost of Slave Labor in the Greco-Roman World." *Ancient Society* 35.1 (2005) 1–17.

Schellenberg, Ryan S. *Abject Joy: Paul, Prison, and the Art of Making Do.* Oxford: Oxford University Press, 2021.

Schenk, Wolfgang. "Der Brief des Paulus an Philemon in der neueren Forschung (1945–1987)." In *Aufstieg und Niedergang der römischen Welt,* edited by Wolfgang Haase, vol. 2.25.4, 3439–95. Berlin: Walter de Gruyter, 1987.

Schwab, Günther. *Echtheitskritische Untersuchungen zu den vier kleinen Paulusbriefen.* Vol. 1A. Norderstedt: Books on Demand, 2011.

Bibliography

Schweitzer, Albert. *Paul and His Interpreters*. Translated by W. Montgomery. London: A. and C. Black, 1912.

Seesengood, Robert. *Philemon: An Introduction and Study Guide*. London: Bloomsbury, 2017.

Seneca. *Epistles 1–65*. Translated by Richard M. Gummere. Loeb Classical Library 75. Cambridge, MA: Harvard University Press, 1917.

Shalev, Eran. *American Zion: The Old Testament as a Political Text from the Revolution to the Civil War*. New Haven, CT: Yale University Press, 2013.

Shaw, Brent. "The Myth of the Neronian Persecution." *Journal of Roman Studies* 105 (2015) 73–100.

Skjønsberg, Anne. *The Jesus Story: Myth or Reality? What do We Know?* Self-published, 2015.

Smith, Ian K. "The Later Pauline Letters: Ephesians, Philippians, Colossians, and Philemon." In *All Things to All Cultures: Paul among Jews, Greeks, and Romans*, edited by Mark Harding and Alanna Nobbs, 302–27. Grand Rapids: Eerdmans, 2013.

Soon, Isaac T. "Before Deception: The Amoral Nature of Ancient Christian Forgery." *Early Christianity* 14.4 (2023) 429–45.

Standhartinger, Angela. "Letter from Prison as Hidden Transcript: What It Tells Us about the People at Philippi." In *The People beside Paul: The Philippian Assembly and History from Below*, edited by Joseph A. Marchal, 107–40. Atlanta: Society of Biblical Literature, 2015.

Steck, Rudolf. "Plinius im Neuen Testament." *Jahrbücher für protestantische Theologie* 17 (1891) 545–84.

Stuhlmacher, Peter. *Der Brief an Philemon*. Evangelisch-Katholischer Kommentar zum Neuen Testament. Zürich: Benziger, 1975.

Suhl, Alfred. *Der Brief an Philemon*. Züricher Bibelkommentare. Zürich: Theologischer Verlag Zürich, 1981.

Tamez, Elsa, Cynthia Briggs Kittredge, Claire Miller Colombo, and Alicia J. Batten. *Philippians, Colossians, Philemon*. Wisdom Commentary. Collegeville, MN: Liturgical, 2017.

Tarazi, Paul Nadim. *Colossians & Philemon*. The Chrysostom Bible. St. Paul, MN: OCABS, 2010.

Theophilos, Michael P. "The Roman Connection: Paul and Mark." In *Paul and Mark: Two Authors at the Beginnings of Christianity*, edited by Oda Wischmeyer , David C. Sim, and Ian J. Elmer, 45–72. Berlin: Walter de Gruyter, 2014.

Thompson, Alan J. *Colossians and Philemon*. Tyndale New Testament Commentaries. Downers Grove, IL: InterVarsity, 2022.

Thompson, James W., and Bruce W. Longenecker. *Philippians and Philemon*. Paideia Commentaries on the New Testament. Grand Rapids: Baker Academic, 2016.

Thompson, Marianne Meye. *Colossians and Philemon*. Two Horizons New Testament Commentary. Grand Rapids: Eerdmans, 2005.

Tite, Philip L. *The Apocryphal Epistle to the Laodiceans: An Epistolary and Rhetorical Analysis*. Leiden: Brill, 2012.

———. "Dusting Off a Pseudo-Historical Letter: Re-Thinking the Epistolary Aspects of the Apocryphal Epistle to the Laodiceans." In *Paul and Pseudepigraphy*, edited by Stanley E. Porter and Gregory P. Fewster, 287–318. Leiden: Brill, 2013.

Trapp, Michael, ed. *Greek and Latin Letters: An Anthology with Translation*. Cambridge: Cambridge University Press, 2003.

Bibliography

Trobisch, David. *Paul's Letter Collection: Tracing the Origins*. Bolivar, MO: Quiet Waters, 2001.

Tuccinardi, Enrico. "An Application of a Profile-Based Method for Authorship Verification: Investigating the Authenticity of Pliny the Younger's Letter to Trajan Concerning the Christians." *Digital Scholarship in the Humanities* 32.2 (2017) 435–47.

Tyson, Joseph B. *Marcion and Luke-Acts: A Defining Struggle*. Columbia: University of South Carolina Press, 2006.

Van den Bergh van Eysinga, G. A. "Christelijke Denkbeelden bij Seneca." *Godsdienst-Wetenschappelijke Studiën* 20 (1956) 35–64.

———. "Edward Evanson." *Nieuw Theologisch Tijdschrift* 2 (1913) 149–64.

———. *La littérature chrétienne primitive*. Paris: F. Rieder, 1926.

———. *De Oudste christelijke Geschriften*. 2 vols. Hague: N. V. Servire, 1946.

———. "Paulus' Brief aan Philemon." *Nieuw Theologisch Tijdschrift* 29 (1940) 1–18.

———. *Radical Views About the New Testament*. Translated by S. B. Slack. Chicago: Open Court, 1912.

Van der Ventel, Brandon I. S., and Richard T. Newman. "Application of the Term Frequency-Inverse Document Frequency Weighting Scheme to the Pauline Corpus." *Andrews University Seminary Studies* 59.2 (2022) 251–71.

Van Manen, W. C. *Handleiding voor de Oudchristelijke Letterkunde*. Leiden: L. Van Nifterik, 1900.

———. *A Wave of Hypercriticism: The English Writings of W. C. van Manen*. Valley, WA: Tellectual, 2014.

Van Nes, Jermo. *Pauline Language and the Pastoral Epistles: A Study of Language Variation in the Corpus Paulinum*. Leiden: Brill, 2017.

Verhoef, Eduard. "The Authenticity of the Paulines Should Not be Assumed." *Protokolle zur Bibel* 19 (2010) 129–51.

———. "Determining the Authenticity of the Paulines." *Journal of Higher Criticism* 11.2 (2005) 83–95.

———. "Die Holländische Radikale Kritik." In *The Corinthian Correspondence*, edited by R. Bieringer, 427–32. Leuven: Peeters/Leuven University Press, 1996.

———. "The 'Dutch Radicals' Espoused Historical Research as the Basic Principle of their Study." In *The Rise of Historical Consciousness Among the Christian Churches*, edited by Kenneth Parker and Erick Moser, 141–60. Lanham, MD: University Press of America, 2013.

———. *Filippenzen, Filemon: Een Praktische Bijbelverklaring*. Teks ten Toelichting. Kampen: Uitgeverij Kok, 1998.

———. "Willem Christiaan van Manen: A Dutch Radical New Testament scholar." *Hervormde Teologiese Studies* 55.1 (1999) 221–7.

Vincent, Marvin R. *A Critical and Exegetical Commentary on the Epistles to the Colossians and to Philemon*. International Critical Commentary. New York: Scribner, 1897.

Von Campenhausen, Hans Freiherr. *Aus der Frühzeit des Christentums: Studien zur Kirchengeschichte des ersten und zweiten Jahrhunderts*. Tübingen: Mohr (Paul Siebeck), 1963.

Von Weizsäcker, Karl. *The Apostolic Age of the Church*. Translated by James Millar. 2nd ed. Oxford: Williams and Norgate, 1895.

Walker, William O. *Interpolations in the Pauline Letters*. Sheffield: Sheffield Academic, 2002.

Bibliography

Wall, Robert W. *Colossians & Philemon*. IVP New Testament Commentary Series. Downers Grove, IL: InterVarsity, 1993.

Walsh, Robyn Faith. *The Origins of Early Christian Literature: Contextualizing the New Testament within Greco-Roman Literary Culture*. Cambridge: Cambridge University Press, 2021.

Weidmann, Frederick W. *Philippians, First and Second Thessalonians, Philemon*. Westminster Bible Companion. Louisville: Westminster John Knox, 2013.

Whittaker, Thomas. *The Origins of Christianity with An Outline of Van Manen's Analysis of the Pauline Literature*. London: Watts, 1904.

Williams, Demetrius K. "'No Longer a Slave': Reading the Interpretation History of Paul's Epistle to Philemon." In *Onesimus Our Brother: Reading Religion, Race, and Culture in Philemon*, edited by Matthew V. Johnson, James A. Noel, and Demetrius K. Williams, 11–45. Minneapolis: Fortress, 2012.

Williams, Travis B. "Textuality and the Dead Sea Scrolls: An Examination of Modern Approaches and Recent Trends." In *The Dead Sea Scrolls and Ancient Media Culture*, edited by Travis B. Williams and Chris Keith, 71–134. Leiden: Brill, 2023.

Wilson, Robert McL. *Colossians and Philemon*. International Critical Commentary. London: T. & T. Clark, 2005.

Wright, N. T. *Colossians and Philemon: An Introduction and Commentary*. Tyndale New Testament Commentaries. Downers Grove, IL: InterVarsity, 1986.

Zeller, E. "Zur Charakteristik der modernen Bekehrungen." *Jahrbücher der Gegenwart* (1845) 14–32.

Zindler, Frank R. *The Jesus the Jews Never Knew: Sepher Toldoth Yeshu and the Quest of the Historical Jesus in Jewish Sources*. Cranford, NJ: American Atheist, 2003.

Zwierlein, Otto. *Petrus in Rom: Die literarischen Zeugnisse*. Berlin: Walter de Gruyter, 2010.

Author Index

Author Index

Scripture Index

1:8	39, 40	7	60, 63, 65, 67
2:21	60	8	60, 63, 64, 94, 95
2:23	60	9	60, 63, 94
4:10	60	10	44, 63, 64, 80
4:11	60	11	60, 68, 91, 101
		12	54, 60, 64

Titus

		13	44, 64, 65
		13–14	92, 95
1:1	20	14	60, 65, 94
1:4	62	15	54, 60, 65
2:2	60	16	54, 63, 64, 65, 66, 95
3:5	84	17	60
3:11	60	18	60, 65
		18–19	95

Philemon

		19	13, 19, 54, 55, 60, 63, 64, 80
1	19, 39, 60, 62–63,	20	60, 64
2	50, 63, 65	21	60, 65
2–3	67	22	43–44, 60, 65, 95
3	62, 63, 65, 66	23	5, 44, 60, 82
4	63, 66	23–24	63, 66
4–5	65	25	48, 66
4–6	8, 59, 63		
4–7	94	James	
5	63, 110	2:21	84
6	63, 65, 67		

9 781666 785005